ALBERTA PLACE NAMES

The Fascinating People & Stories
Behind the Naming of Alberta

LARRY DONOVAN

TOM MONTO

DRAGON
HILL

The Publisher: Dragon Hill Publishing Ltd.

Library and Archives Canada Cataloguing in Publication
Donovan, Larry, 1948–

      Alberta place names: the fascinating people and stories behind the naming of Alberta / Larry Donovan, Tom Monto

ISBN 10: 1-896124-11-9
ISBN 13: 978-1-896124-11-7

    1. Names, Geographical—Alberta. 2. Alberta—History, Local. I. Monto, Tom, 1961– II. Title

FC3656.D65 2007   917.123001'4   C2006-906627-2

Project Director: Gary Whyte

Project Editor: Tom Monto

PC: P5

CONTENTS

INTRODUCTION

One of the things that struck me as I helped write this book was the incredible range of Alberta place names. From the quaint Beaumont to the grotesque Gargoyle Mountain...from the familial Millicent to the corporate Nacmine...from the mineral Blackstone River to the animal Wapiti Mountain. The range is truly mind-boggling.

Alberta place names come from a variety of languages, too. From English, there is Edmonton; from Galician, Wostok; from Chinese, Ha-Ling; from Cree, Wetaskiwin. The source of the place names range from war, Mons Peak, to peace, Peace River; from the small, Little Smoky, to the large, Okotoks, named after what is said to be the largest erratic in the world.

Some names come from the smallest of happenings, such as Pincher Creek; some from the largest. For example, the world wars gave us the names for Mount Kitchener and Mount Bazalgette and many other places. Some names come from the feature's colour, such as Vermilion; some from its shape, Roche Ronde; some from its temperature, Cold Lake; some from its sound, Hell-Roaring Falls.

Some place names come from the location, real or imagined, such as Noral, Fifth Meridian and One-Four. Some are slang, Nojack; some are formal, Duchess and Empress. Some place names are humorous, Kicking Horse Pass; some critical, Storm Mountain; some positive, Utopian; some utopian, Paradise Valley. Alberta has a Royalties, a Black Diamond, a Leather Peak, and an Arrowwood, representing resources used through time. With the addition of a Silicon Valley, the historical series would be right up to date.

There are those features noticeable in their aloneness, Netook, Lost Mountain and Lone Mountain, and those who seem to find warmth in good company, for example, Valley of the Ten Peaks, two of which, Wenkchemna and Neptuak, are known only by their numbers.

Many Alberta place names memorialize people, crops and foods. Wheatland is from the farm side of life, while Millet is misleadingly not derived from the crop of that name, but instead from a French painter. Although Sunset Peak is straightforward, named after a sun setting over it, Rainbow Lake may have been given its name because it is shaped like a rainbow, or perhaps it was named after a person, Rainbow Fournier. Scientists are remembered in Mount Blakiston and Mount Sullivan, as are politicians in Breton, Boyle and Scotford. The name of Mount Bess remembers a woman who would marry a politician; the name Parlby remembers a man who would do the same. A good cook is remembered in Delia, a critical lack of food in Fitzgerald. Cooks who boil when they cook are remembered in the name Mount Assiniboine.

Some place names are Christian, Mount Chown and Cloister Mountain; some harken to the Islamic, Alhambra; some are derived from Native spirituality, Sundance; some are from the dark side, Devils Head and Lake Minnewanka. Alberta place names range from the down and dirty, Hairy Hill, to the mysterious, Mystery Lake and Seven Persons, and to the literary, with places named after British publisher Blackie, authors Balzac and Bindloss and the fictional character Carvel.

The Crimean War gave us Nightingale and Mount Dalhousie. The Boer War gave us Mount Botha, named after a Boer military commander who fought against Baden-Powell's "boy scouts" at Ladysmith and captured war correspondent Winston Churchill, who later became a British prime minister.

Speaking of Nightingale, two other place names remember those who risked their lives to aid others, Mount Edith Cavell and Mount Scrimger. The name of another feature, Mount Bergne, remembers a good climbing buddy after his tragic death.

There are names reminiscent of the pre-historic, Dinosaur Park; of the ancient, Mount Chephren; of the historic, Bon Accord; of the old, Calgary; and of the new, Municipality of Crowsnest Pass.

Although many of these place names are relatively recent imports from faraway lands and cultures, the timeless land we know as Alberta has survived through countless winters and summers, running through its seasonal cycles millions of times, providing timeless low-tech beauty in such places as Punchbowl Falls and Cascade Mountain. This timelessness lends credibility to such names as Eon Mountain.

Alphabetically the names stretch from Abee to Zigadenus Lake. Alberta place names start with every letter of the alphabet except x. This book arranges the place names according to how they are commonly known, with The Castelets under Castelets, Mount Allen under Mount, Lac la Biche under Lac and St. Albert under Saint.

I hope you find reading about these place names as interesting as I found researching this book.

A

ABBOT PASS (2922 m) This pass was named after Phillip Stanley Abbot. He was a member of the Appalachian Mountain Club and fell to his death in 1896 on the second ascent of Mount Lefroy. Abbot Pass is about 55 km west-northwest of Banff.

ABEE Pop. 32. The hamlet of Abee was named after A.B. Donnelly, a manager with the Northwest Lumber Company, Edmonton. Abee is approximately 86 km northeast of Edmonton.

ACME Pop. 661. The village of Acme, located about 63 km northeast of Calgary, took its name from the Greek word *acme,* meaning "summit." Before 1909, Acme was known as Tapscott Post Office.

AETNA One of the hills surrounding the hamlet of Aetna reminded John W. Taylor of Mount Etna, a volcanic mountain in eastern Sicily. Taylor, a senior authority of the Mormon Church in Salt Lake City, Utah, named the settlement in 1893. The spelling was a slight deviation from the original Etna. Aetna is located about 68 km southwest of Lethbridge. It was a thriving Mormon community in the early 1900s and supported a school, a cheese factory and other businesses.

AIRDRIE Pop. 29,035. Shadowed by nearby sister city Calgary, Airdrie took pride that its name likely had its origin in antiquity…something Calgary cannot boast. Airdrie was founded in 1889 and was named after Airdrie, Strathclyde, Scotland. The origin of the Scottish place name has been the subject of controversy among writers and historians. Some suggest the name comes from air-dry, referring to

A

atmospheric conditions. Others say the name is Celtic for "high level," a view rejected by others who say Airdrie in Scotland may stand high, but it has no level part. Also rejected is an interpretation that the name means "high pasture run." Historians of the Scottish community are now satisfied that *airdrie* means "The King's Height." It is possible the rising ground upon which Airdrie, Scotland stands was the scene of the Battle of Arderytn in 577 AD between Aeddan, King of Kintire, and Rydderich the Bountiful, King of Strathclwyd.

ALBERTA Pop. 3,306,359. As a provisional district in the North-West Territories, Alberta was named in 1882 by Governor General Marquess of Lorne, after his wife, Princess Louise Caroline Alberta. She was the fourth daughter of Queen Victoria. Alberta became a province in 1905 through an act of the Canadian Parliament. At this time, Alberta grew to include the west half of the NWT district of Athabaska, which extended north to the 60th parallel, and a thin strip on the west edge of the old NWT districts of Saskatchewan and Assiniboia.

ALBERTA BEACH Pop. 640. This summer village 60 km west of Edmonton was named by the Canadian Northern Railway after the province of Alberta. Incorporated in 1920, Alberta Beach is a resort on the southeast shores of Lac Ste. Anne.

ALDER FLATS Pop. 139. This hamlet was named after the alder trees found in the area. Alder Flats is approximately 32 km south of Drayton Valley.

ALDERSYDE The hamlet of Aldersyde derived its name from *Aldersyde*, a fictional story written by Annie Swan in 1927. Aldersyde is about 40 km southeast of Calgary.

ALEXANDER INDIAN RESERVE Pop. 804. In 1882, this Cree reserve about 52 km west of Edmonton was established and named after Chief Alexander Arcand.

A

ALHAMBRA The name for this hamlet likely comes from John T. Moore. He was president of the local Alberta Central Railway and jestingly wanted to create a mental connection between the railway community and the ancient palace and fortress in Granada, Spain, once occupied by Moorish kings. Before getting this grandiose name, the local post office was called Horseguards. Alhambra is located 18 km east of Rocky Mountain House.

ALIX Pop. 775. Incorporated as a village in 1907, this community 45 km east-northeast of Red Deer was named after an early settler and rancher in the area, Alexia "Alix" Westhead.

MORE ABOUT ALIX…*One woman who had an impact on Alix, Alberta and Canada was Mary Irene Marryat. She was eligible for a life of ease in the British aristocracy but found her niche in the open spaces surrounding the central Alberta community of Alix. She met and married Alberta farmer Walter Parlby, an Oxford graduate who shared her interests in literature and theatre (and for whom Parlby Creek was named). The young Irene Parlby turned heads in Alix with her varied tastes and abilities—she liked pretty clothes and fine china but also enjoyed bronco riding and buckskins. She grew fond of the community and started women's groups for mutual assistance and self-education. These groups were the forerunners of the United Farm Women of Alberta. When the United Farmers of Alberta (UFA) became a political party, Parlby was asked to run for office in the Lacombe riding. She was elected to office in 1921 and served as a cabinet minister in the UFA cabinet, the first woman cabinet minister in the province and the second in the whole British Empire. In the Alberta Legislature, she put through legislation that improved the lives of women and children. She was a member of the "Famous Five" in the Persons Case, a legal battle that went to the Privy Council in England and upheld that women were indeed persons and eligible for appointment to the Senate.*

A

ALLIANCE Pop. 169. This village 45 km northwest of Coronation grew up around a Canadian Northern Railway siding. The siding was named Alliance by railway land agent Tom Edwards after his hometown in Ohio.

ALLISON PEAK (2643 m) In 1915 this peak was named in the memory of Douglas Allison. He served in the Royal North-West Mounted Police before becoming an early settler in the area. Allison Peak is near Coleman. Locals sometimes refer to this peak as the Needle's Eye.

ALTARIO The name for this hamlet is a combination of Alberta and Ontario. A post office opened here in 1919 and was called Wilhelmina before the area was renamed Altario. The community is located about 48 km south of Provost.

AMBER MOUNTAIN (2542 m) This is a descriptive name for this mountain. Its summit has yellowish-coloured shale. Amber Mountain is 16 km southeast of Jasper.

AMBER VALLEY First known as Pine Creek, this locality near Athabasca is a pioneer black community, settled by people from the southern United States in the early 1900s. Around 1932, residents petitioned for a post office, and a local teacher suggested the name Amber Valley because of the yellow colour of the soil.

AMISK Pop. 214. Established as a post office in 1908, this village got its name from the Cree word for "beaver." It is assumed the name was chosen because of the many beaver in the area. Amisk was incorporated as a village in 1956. It is located southeast of Hardisty.

ANDERSON PEAK (2652 m) This peak was named after Lieutenant Samuel Anderson (1839–81), of the Royal Engineers. He was the chief astronomer in the British complement of the North American Boundary Commission (1872–74). The Commission defined the Canada–U.S. border from the Lake

A

of the Woods to the Rocky Mountains. Anderson Peak is near Waterton Lakes National Park.

ANDREW Pop. 484. A post office was opened here in 1902 and took the name of Andrew Whitford, one of the first homesteaders in the district. Andrew was incorporated as a village in 1930. Andrew is 29 km southeast of Smoky Lake.

ANGEL GLACIER This is a descriptive name for the glacier located near Jasper, whose shape resembles that of an angel.

ANTHOZOAN MOUNTAIN (2695 m) This mountain, about 45 km northwest of Banff, was named after the anthozoan coral reefs preserved in the mountain's Devonian limestone.

ANZAC Pop. 297. The name for this hamlet is an abbreviation of the World War I Australian and New Zealand Army Corps. Anzac is about 35 km southeast of Fort McMurray.

APEX MOUNTAIN (3250 m) The name is descriptive of the mountain's appearance. Apex Mountain is located about 75 km southeast of Jasper.

APPARITION MOUNTAIN (3002 m) The name for this mountain is consistent with other names in the vicinity. For some time the area has had a paranormal undercurrent that is reflected in many of its place names, such as Devils Head, Ghost River and Phantom Crag. Apparition Mountain is near Banff.

AQUILA MOUNTAIN (2825 m) *Aquila* is Latin for "eagle." When this mountain was named in 1916, an eagle was seen at its peak. Aquila Mountain is 16 km south of Jasper.

ARCTOMYS PEAK (2793 m) This peak, approximately 130 km northwest of Banff, took its name from *Arctomys columbianus*, the genus name of the whistling marmots found in the valley.

A

ARCTURUS PEAK (2447 m) Part of the Starlight Range, Arcturus Peak is 74 km northwest of Jasper. This peak was named after a character from Greek mythology—Arcturus, the son of Zeus and Callisto. *Arcturus* is the Greek word for "little bear."

ARDENODE Major George Davis named this hamlet after a village in Ireland. Ardenode, 42 km east of Calgary, started as a railway siding around 1911.

ARDMORE Pop. 239. This hamlet near Cold Lake was named after the local school district of Ardmore. The name of the school district was chosen by one of the area's early settlers, Mr. Whilley. The name was the name of his Oklahoma hometown. That United States community had been named after Ardmore, Ireland. The name means "great height."

ARDROSSAN Pop. 176. This hamlet was named after Ardrossan, Ayrshire, Scotland. The name is from the Gaelic and means "height of the little cape." Ardrossan, near Edmonton, was named by Miss Edmiston, a local resident.

ARGENTIA BEACH Pop. 4. This summer village (incorporated in 1967) was first named Silver Bay, but the name was changed to Argentia Beach to avoid confusion with Silver Beach on Pigeon Lake. The name comes from the Latin word *argentums,* meaning "silver." Argentia Beach is 46 km west-northwest of Wetaskiwin.

ARIES PEAK (2996 m) *Aries* is the Latin word for "ram." A.O. Wheeler named this mountain after the mountain sheep in the area. Aries Peak is about 100 km northwest of Banff.

ARMENA Pop. 48. This hamlet had its beginning in 1911 as a railway station for the Canadian Northern Railway. Before that, the district was called Thodenskjold, a name difficult to spell and pronounce according to some in the

A

area. A group wrote to a government department in Edmonton requesting a new name for the community. They received word that the name Armena could be used. The name's origin is not known. Armena is near Camrose.

ARRIS MOUNTAIN (2705 m) M.P. Bridgland, the namesake of Mount Bridgland, named this mountain near Jasper after its rugged shape. An arris, like an arête, is a sharp edge or ridge.

ARROWWOOD Pop. 170. This village 68 km southeast of Calgary took its name from the nearby East and West Arrowhead creeks. Natives made arrows from the short willow bushes that grew in abundance on the banks of the creeks. In 1909, the post office situated on the East Arrowwood Creek was named Arrowwood, and the name passed to the village that grew there.

ASHMOUNT Pop. 176. L.W. Babcock, the first postmaster in the area, named the post office after a suburb of Boston, Massachusetts, where he had lived. The hamlet of Ashmount is about 55 km southwest of Bonnyville.

ASPEN BEACH The locality of Aspen Beach, at one time a summer village, is located near Lacombe on the shores of Gull Lake. Aspen Beach was named for the aspen trees commonly found there. The community's post office, previously known as Wiesville, operated from 1916 to 1973.

ASSUMPTION The area's post office acquired its name from its location in the rectory of the Our Lady of Assumption Indian School on the Hay Lake Indian Reserve. In 1970, the post office name was changed to Chateh at the request of the Band council. However, the hamlet retained the name Assumption. Assumption is located northwest of High Level.

A

ASTORIA PASS (2316 m) This pass was named after the fur traders based in NWC post Astoria who crossed Athabasca Pass in 1814. Fort Astoria, located on the Columbia River, had been set up by John Jacob Astor's Pacific Fur Company three years earlier. The fur trading post and the fur company were purchased by the North West Company in 1813. Astoria Pass is near Jasper.

ATHABASCA Pop. 2313. The town of Athabasca is about 150 km north of Edmonton, on the banks of the Athabasca River. The Hudson's Bay Company established a trading post and transit point here in 1848. Athabasca Landing saw thousands of tonnes of goods shipped by boat to the Mackenzie River valley via Lake Athabasca. The centre's importance as a distribution/collection centre for goods and furs from the north and south decreased after various railways were built to the area in the early 1900s. In 1911, Athabasca was incorporated as a town, with the word "landing" being dropped from its name at that time. Athabasca University, Alberta's first distance-learning university, moved from Edmonton to the town in 1984.

ATHABASCA PASS (1737 m) The first recorded crossing of this pass, about 55 km south of Jasper, was made by David Thompson in 1811. The pass was probably named for its proximity to the head of the Athabasca River. Athabasca Pass is on the Continental Divide and was used for many years by fur traders crossing the Rocky Mountains. This pass, with its grand and rugged scenery, was less often used after Canada's first transcontinental railway was completed through the Rockies by way of the Kicking Horse Pass and Rogers Pass.

ATHABASCA RIVER, ATHABASCA FALLS, ATHABASCA GLACIER, LAKE ATHABASCA, MOUNT ATHABASCA It is generally accepted that *Athabasca* is the Cree word for "a place where there are reeds." The name refers to the reeds that grow in the delta of the Athabasca

A

River at Lake Athabasca. Lake Athabasca, 260 km northeast of Fort McMurray, played an important role in the early fur trade. Northern traders from the Arctic and traders from the Pacific met at Fort Chipewyan on the shores of the lake. About 32 km from Jasper, Athabasca River passes over the Athabasca Falls. Athabasca Glacier and Mount Athabasca (3491 m) are so named for their closeness to this river. An alternate spelling, Athabaska, was also used for these features until 1948 when Athabasca became official.

ATIKAMEG Pop. 338. This hamlet took its name from the Cree word for "whitefish." Atikameg is about 90 km northwest of Slave Lake.

AURORA MOUNTAIN (2970 m). Aurora Mountain was named after a World War I British warship that took part in a 1915 battle in the North Sea. Aurora Mountain is about 100 km southwest of Calgary.

B

BADLANDS, THE This is a descriptive name for the area along the lower course of the Red Deer River. The exact origin of the name is not known, but it is believed the area's rugged topography and aridity gave rise to the name. In the Badlands, erosion has revealed layers of rock from different geological eras, exposing many dinosaur fossils. Fossilized oyster beds have also been found, pointing to marine life in the area in a long-ago age. Having hoodoos and other unusual-looking geological formations, the area resembles another world.

BALZAC This hamlet 18 km north of Calgary was named by Sir William Cornelius Van Horne, then president of the CPR, after Honoré de Balzac (1799–1850), the noted 19th-century French novelist who in 20 years wrote 85 novels. In 1912, the local post office opened under the name Beddington and changed its name to Balzac in 1925.

BANDED PEAK (2934 m) This descriptive name refers to the bands of differently coloured rock near the mountain's peak. Banded Peak is 45 km west of Turner Valley.

BANFF Pop. 6098. This town is the focus of one of the best-known international tourist destinations in the world, Banff National Park. It took its name from Banffshire, Scotland. Banff comes from the Gaelic word *bunnaimb*, meaning "mouth of the river." When the transcontinental railway was built through the area, the CPR established a siding, Siding 29, near the present townsite. In 1905, the community was renamed Banff by Lord Strathcona. It is 90 km west of Calgary.

B

MORE ABOUT BANFF NATIONAL PARK...*It has been declared a World Heritage Site by the United Nations Educational Scientific and Cultural Organization (UNESCO). It is a World Heritage Site for good reason. Banff National Park runs 240 km along the eastern slope of the Continental Divide. It is one of the most spectacular parks in the world, containing magnificent Rocky Mountain peaks, glacial lakes, rivers, meadows and a vast wilderness. Some 700 species of plants and about 240 species of birds have been recorded in Banff National Park. The forests are home to moose, elk, deer, mountain sheep, cougars, wolves, black bears and the grizzly bear. Elk and bighorn sheep are often seen near or in the townsite of Banff.*

In 1885, a 25-square-kilometre area was set aside as a reserve for public use following the discovery of sulphur mineral hot springs at what has become known as the Cave and Basin. Since then, the hot springs reserve has grown into a national park that is 6640 square kilometres in area. Banff National Park attracts about four million visitors a year. Some of the visitors visit the world-famous Banff Centre School of Fine Arts.

BARBETTE MOUNTAIN (3072 m) This name refers to the mountain's resemblance to a barbette, a gun platform used by naval guns. Barbette Mountain is 95 km northwest of Banff.

BARIL PEAK (2998 m) This peak was named after M.C.L. Baril of the Surveyor General's staff. He was killed in action in 1915 during World War I. Baril Peak is about 52 km southwest of Turner Valley.

BARNES RIDGE This ridge near Calgary is likely named after E.C. Barnes, an early homesteader in the area.

BARNWELL Pop. 552. Founded in 1902 by four Mormon pioneers, this village was named for Richard Barnwell, a purchasing agent for the Canadian Pacific Railway. It was

B

previously called Woodpecker after nearby Woodpecker Island in the Oldman River. Barnwell is located about 40 km east of Lethbridge.

BARONS Pop. 285. This village was named after Baron, a high-ranking official in the Canadian Pacific Railway, which bought the townsite in 1909. The village's Union Bank branch adopted the name Baron's Bank, and other businesses began using the possessive form of the name. To follow local usage, the CPR officially added the "s" to Baron a short time later. Before 1909, the local post office was known as Blayney.

BARRHEAD Pop. 4239. The town of Barrhead got its name from Barrhead, Scotland, the birthplace of James McGuire, an early settler in the district. *Barr* is the Gaelic word for "top." Barrhead is located about 89 km northwest of Edmonton.

BARRICADE MOUNTAIN (2593 m) This name is descriptive of the mountain, which sports a ridge resembling a barricade. Barricade Mountain is 112 km northwest of Jasper.

BARRIER MOUNTAIN (2957 m) This mountain forms a ridge separating the Panther River and the Red Deer River. Barrier Mountain is 55 km north of Banff.

BASELINE MOUNTAIN (height unknown) This mountain took its name from its location on the Tenth Baseline of the Dominion Land Survey system, at exactly 52°8' North, 345 km (or 216 miles) north of the Canada–U.S. border. Baseline Mountain is about 42 km southwest of Rocky Mountain House.

BASHAW Pop. 775. This town 48 km south of Camrose was named after Eugene Bashaw. He owned land where the town is located. Before 1910, its post office was called Forster.

B

BASILICA MOUNTAIN (2865 m) This mountain near Jasper was named for its apparent resemblance to a basilica.

BASSANO Pop. 1272. This town was named after the Marquis de Bassano, a major shareholder in the Canadian Pacific Railway. Bassano is the site of the second largest dam of its kind in the world—only the Aswan Dam in Egypt is larger. Bassano is located 125 km southeast of Calgary.

BASTION PEAK (2970 m) This mountain with its sharp peak has the appearance of a bastion. Bastion Peak is about 26 km southwest of Jasper.

BATEMAN RIDGE This ridge was named after Tom Bateman, a rancher in the area. Bateman Ridge is near Calgary.

BATTLE CREEK An 1873 massacre at this site in the Cypress Hills pushed Prime Minister John A. Macdonald to establish the North-West Mounted Police. A group of Assiniboine led by Chief Little Soldier was camped alongside the creek, drinking rotgut whisky bought from a nearby trading post, when some U.S. wolfers met up with them and accused the group of stealing some of their horses. The ensuing battle left 36 Assiniboine dead. The incident became known as the Cypress Hills Massacre. Battle Creek is about 60 km southeast of Medicine Hat.

BAWLF Pop. 364. The village of Bawlf southeast of Camrose took the name of Nicholas Bawlf, president of the North Elevator Company and of the Winnipeg Grain Exchange, in 1907. Its post office was formerly known as Molstand.

BEACON PEAK (2986 m) This is a descriptive name for the isolated peak that resembles a beacon. Beacon Peak is approximately 39 km south-southwest of Jasper.

B

BEARSPAW This former hamlet was named after Chief Masgwaahsid, which translates as "bear's paw." He signed Treaty 7 at Blackfoot Crossing on the Bow River in 1877. Bearspaw is near Calgary.

BEAUMONT Pop. 6518 The name for this town south of Edmonton is French for "a beautiful mountain." It was named in 1895 and is located on a hill surrounded by flat prairie. Beaumont was incorporated as a town in 1973.

BEAUVALLON The name is French for "a beautiful valley" and is well suited for this hamlet along the Vermilion River. The post office opened in this hamlet near Two Hills in 1909.

BEAVERLODGE Pop. 1997. This town in the Peace River district took its name from the nearby Beaverlodge River. The name Beaverlodge is a translation of the Native Beaver language word *Uz-i-pa*, with the word "lodge" meaning "a temporary dwelling." In 1908 the first white settlers came to the area and, pending the first official land survey, "squatted" in the valley getting their mail at the Redwillow Post Office. The Edmonton, Dunvegan and British Columbia Railway, which arrived in 1928, established a new townsite under the name Beaverlodge about two km from the old post office.

BEAZER This hamlet was named in honour of Mark Beazer (?–1937), the local postmaster and Mormon bishop. Beazer is 80 km southwest of Lethbridge.

BEEHIVE MOUNTAIN (2895 m) This is a descriptive name for this mountain, located about 75 km southwest of Turner Valley.

BEISEKER Pop. 781. This village was named after Thomas Beiseker of Fessenden, North Dakota, one of the owners of the Calgary Colonization Company. In the early 1900s, the company purchased 1000 square kilometres of land in the Calgary area for resale to immigrants from the U.S.

B

and other farmers. Beiseker, said to be one of the wealthiest men in North Dakota, owned about 40 banks. He lost his fortune in the 1920s, but not before he donated land for the townsite of Beiseker when a CPR rail line was established there. The community is located 50 km northeast of Calgary.

BELLEVUE This former village in the Crowsnest Pass was named in 1905 by J.J. Fleutot, of the Western Canadian Collieries. Bellevue's name comes from the view provided by its scenic mountain setting. In French, *bellevue* means "a good view." In 1979, Bellevue was consolidated with other communities in the Crowsnest Pass to form the Municipality of Crowsnest Pass. (see Crowsnest Pass)

BELLIS This hamlet 23 km northeast of Smoky Lake got its name from *beei lis*, an approximation of the Ukrainian word for "white poplar trees." It became a village in 1928 but is now a hamlet.

BELLY RIVER The Belly River lies northwest of Lethbridge and flows into the Oldman River. There are different versions of how the Belly River received its name. It may be named after the Atsina, a splinter tribe of the Arapaho that was known by the French as the *Gros Ventres*, meaning "big bellies." The Arapaho called them *hitunena*, meaning "beggars," which the French may have incorrectly translated as "belly people." On the other hand, perhaps the name describes the large bend, or belly, in the river.

BENALTO Pop. 100. This hamlet got its name from two words. *Ben* is Gaelic for "a hill," and *alto* is the Latin word for "high." The two words were combined to form the name. The community is located 32 km west of Red Deer.

BENNINGTON PEAK (3265 m) A.O. Wheeler named this peak in 1922 after Bennington, Vermont, the birthplace of explorer and fur trader Simon Fraser. Bennington Peak is 29 km southwest of Jasper. (see Mount Fraser)

B

BENTLEY Pop. 987. This village was named after George Bentley, who operated a sawmill in the district. It was incorporated as a village in 1915. Bentley is located 28 km northwest of Red Deer.

BERWYN This village was named after the Berwyn Hills in Wales. The name comes from the Welsh words *bar*, meaning "summit," and *gwyn* or *wyn*, meaning "white," creating a suitable name for the snow-covered hills there. Before 1922, the Alberta community was situated five km east of its present location and was named Bear Lake. That year it moved to the end-of-steel of the Edmonton, Dunvegan and British Columbia Railway. Berwyn is near Grimshaw.

BETULA BEACH Pop. 8. This summer village 40 km northeast of Drayton Valley got its name from the birch trees in the area. *Betula* is the Latin word for "birch."

BEZANSON Pop. 72. This hamlet was named in honour of one of the pioneers of the Peace River country. A. Maynard Bezanson (1878–1958) took a leading role in the development of the district and promoted the townsite. Bezanson is 30 km northeast of Grande Prairie.

BIDENT MOUNTAIN (3084 m) This mountain took its descriptive name from its resemblance to a double tooth. Bident Mountain is located 45 km northwest of Banff.

BIG COULEE Big Coulee is located 20 km northeast of Athabasca. The origin of the name is uncertain, although it is probably a descriptive term.

BIG HILL SPRINGS PROVINCIAL PARK This park, located about 30 km northwest of Calgary, took its name from a spring on a large hill in the area. At one time, Aboriginal people camped near the spring and used the big hill as a buffalo jump to kill bison.

BIG KNIFE PROVINCIAL PARK This park 40 km northeast of Stettler took its name from a confrontation between Big Man, a Cree, and Knife, a Blackfoot. According to legend, both men lost their lives in the fight.

BIG VALLEY Pop. 308. The name for this village is descriptive of the wide, open valley that runs from Ewing Lake to the Red Deer River. Big Valley is 33 km south of Stettler.

BIGHORN RANGE This mountain range near Nordegg took its name from the abundance of Rocky Mountain sheep, or bighorn sheep, in the area.

BINDLOSS This hamlet north of Medicine Hat was named after once-popular English novelist Harold Bindloss (1866–1945). He used Alberta and the Canadian West for the settings of many of his novels. Bindloss lived in western Canada for some time before returning to England in 1896.

BINGLEY PEAK (2438 m) This mountain was named after the English birthplace of noted traveller Dr. William Cheadle. He accompanied Viscount Milton across the empty Canadian West in 1862 and 1863. Bingley Peak is about 36 km west of Jasper. (see Cheadle)

BIRCHAM Pop. 9. It is thought this locality was named after Bircham, King's Lynn, England. It is approximately 60 km northeast of Calgary.

BITTERN LAKE Pop. 193. The name for this village was derived from the name of the nearby lake. The lake got its name from its Cree name *mokakasiu,* after the large number of bitterns on the lakeshore. (A bittern is similar to a heron but smaller. It inhabits reedy marshes.) Bittern Lake is near Camrose.

B

BITUMOUNT The locality of Bitumount is about 73 km northwest of Fort McMurray. In 1922, A.W. Wheeler started to experiment with extracting oil from the tar sands at that location. He called his extraction plant Alcan Oil Co., and he named the post office after himself. In 1927, the company changed hands, and the new owner, R.C. Fitzsimmons, renamed the operation International Bitumen Co. Later, in 1934, he changed the name of the post office to Bitumount. The early extraction methods were slow, and efficient extraction of synthetic oil from the tar sands did not begin until Dr. Karl Clark's breakthroughs in the 1930s.

MORE ABOUT BITUMOUNT... *Today, the tar sands in northern Alberta fill a significant amount of Canada's synthetic crude oil requirements. Dr. Karl Clark did pioneering work in unlocking the oil from the tar sands. In 1920, he joined the newly formed Research Council of Alberta and looked for ways to use oil sands for paving roads. His research evolved into developing a technique that could separate oil from the sand. His "water flotation extraction method" involves mixing tar sands with hot water and then taking off the bitumen tar when it rises to the surface. The tar undergoes an extraction and refining process to yield synthetic crude oil. With the start of World War II and the increased demand for oil, the federal government constructed an extraction plant at Bitumount. Dr. Clark's hot water process proved successful and eventually caught the attention of major oil companies. Great Canadian Oil Sands (G.C.O.S.) completed the first commercial facility in 1967. Unfortunately, Dr. Clark never saw G.C.O.S. go into operation because he had died the previous year.*

BLACK CAT MOUNTAIN (2462 m) This mountain appears to have the profile of a startled cat with its distinctive arched back. Black Cat Mountain is near Hinton.

B

BLACK DIAMOND Pop. 1811. This town was named in 1907 after nearby coal mines on the Sheep River. The Black Diamond Coal Mine was opened by Addison McPherson (1846–1929), who suggested the post office should have the same name as his coal mine. Black Diamond is near Turner Valley.

BLACK ROCK MOUNTAIN (2462 m) This mountain is about 30 km north-northeast of Canmore. Its descriptive name comes from its sharp, black peak.

BLACKFALDS Pop. 1811. The town of Blackfalds is 12 km north of Red Deer. The locality was originally named Waghorn, and the nearby siding on the Calgary & Edmonton Railway was simply named 11th Siding. The name was changed in 1902 to Blackfalds by a Canadian Pacific Railway engineer who thought the area resembled his home, Blackfalds, Scotland.

BLACKFOOT This hamlet near Lloydminster took its name from the nearby Blackfoot Hills. These hills were hunting grounds for the Blackfoot and also were the scene of many battles between the Blackfoot and the Cree.

BLACKIE This hamlet was named after John Stuart Blackie, a Scottish professor, novelist and founder of the publishing company Blackie and Sons. Blackie is 50 km southeast of Calgary.

BLACKSTONE RIVER This river north of Nordegg was named for the shale at its headwater.

BLAIRMORE Pop. 6500. In 1898, the Canadian Pacific Railway named this former town in the Crowsnest Pass after Andrew G. Blair (1844–1907). Blair had served as the premier of New Brunswick and was at the time minister of Railways and Canals in the federal government. Apparently, some in the community said Blair was too short a name, and that more should be added. So "more"

B

was added, making the name Blairmore. Others contend the town was named after two contractors (Mr. Blair and Mr. More) who laid the CPR line through Blairmore. In 1979, Blairmore and other Crowsnest Pass communities were consolidated to form the Municipality of Crowsnest Pass. (see Crowsnest Pass)

BLINDMAN RIVER A group of Cree hunters overcome with snow blindness camped on the river until their sight recovered. They gave this river near Red Deer its name.

BLUE RIDGE Pop. 274. This hamlet took its descriptive name from the blue haze that is often seen on a nearby ridge. Blue Ridge is 20 km east of Whitecourt.

BLUEROCK MOUNTAIN (2789 m) The name describes the colour of this mountain near Turner Valley.

BLUESKY Pop. 197. This hamlet took its name from the cloudless skies that are characteristic of the area. Bluesky is near Fairview.

BLUFF MOUNTAIN (2145 m) This mountain near Blairmore is reminiscent of a bluff, a steep cliff or bank.

BLUFFTON Pop. 144. The name for this hamlet is derived from bluff, the Canadian Prairie word for "a grove of trees," many of which are found in the area. Bluffton is near Rimbey.

BODO This hamlet about 25 km south-southeast of Provost was named after Bodo, a community in northern Norway. Originally the Alberta community was called Scheck.

BONAR This locality near Hanna is believed to be named after Andrew Bonar Law. Born in New Brunswick, he was prime minister of Britain from 1922 to 1923. Bonar Law was the first British prime minister to be born outside of the UK.

B

BON ACCORD Pop. 1493. This town north of Edmonton took its name from the motto of the city of Aberdeen, Scotland. *Bon accord*, meaning "perfect harmony," was used as a password in 1308 when Aberdonians, inspired by Robert the Bruce, took up arms against the city's English garrison and killed every one of the soldiers. The name Bon Accord suggested by former Aberdonian Alexander "Sandy" Florence, was accepted as the name of the new Alberta public school district in 1896. The name was later adopted by the post office and the community.

BONDISS Pop. 120. This summer village is 40 km southeast of Athabasca. The exact origin of the name is not known. Bondiss was incorporated in 1983.

BONNET PEAK (3136 m) This name describes the shape of the mountain's summit. Bonnet Peak is about 36 km northwest of Banff.

BONNYVILLE Pop. 5397. This town was named in honour of Oblate Father F.S. Bonny. After serving as a missionary in Africa, Father Bonny established the first Roman Catholic church in the Bonnyville area in 1910. Bonnyville is 122 km northwest of Lloydminster.

BONNYVILLE BEACH Pop. 64. This summer village was named for its closeness to Bonnyville.

BOTHA Pop. 194. This village 12 km southeast of Stettler was named after Louis Botha (1862–1919). He was a moderate Boer with a cooperative attitude toward British immigrants in South Africa, but during the Boer War, he became a Boer general and led the fighting against the British army. After the war, he was the first prime minister of the Union of South Africa.

BOTTREL This hamlet 50 km northwest of Calgary was named after an early settler of the area, Edward Botterel.

B

The different spelling is attributed to an error made by an Ottawa official.

BOW CITY This former hamlet 92 km northeast of Lethbridge never realized the dreams of developers who saw promise in the large seam of coal nearby on the banks of the Bow River. Speculators came to the area and drove up real estate prices. Their expectations were riding on proposed plans for major expansion of the railways to carry coal to Hudson Bay and to points in the United States. But the start of World War I saw capital investment decline for the community's various developments. The growth of the community, once expected to rival Calgary, fizzled. Over the years, as the demand for coal lessened, businesses and residents moved away from Bow City. In 1966, the Bow City Post Office closed.

BOW ISLAND Pop. 1688. This town 54 km southwest of Medicine Hat was named after a nearby island in the Bow River.

BOW PASS (2042 m) This pass is about 90 km northwest of Banff. (see Bow River)

BOW RIVER This river starts at Bow Glacier and flows into Bow Lake, through the eastern slopes of the Rocky Mountains and across the southern prairies before joining with the Oldman River to form the South Saskatchewan River. According to J.B. Tyrrell, it took its name from its Cree name *ma-na-cha-ban sipi*, meaning "the place where wood for bows is taken." Its banks grew wood that was suitable for making bows.

BOWDEN Pop. 1014. There are a number of theories as to how this town 42 km southwest of Red Deer was named. Perhaps it was named after a place near Manchester, England. On the other hand, the town may be named for Bowden, Scotland. The most accepted account is that a surveyor, one Mr. Williamson, requested that this

B

siding take the maiden name of his wife. The town was incorporated in September 1981.

BOWELL This former hamlet was named after Sir Mackenzie Bowell (1823–1917), who served as Canada's prime minister from 1894 to 1896. Bowell is near Medicine Hat.

BOYLE Pop. 868. This village was named for John Robert Boyle, who served as a Liberal member of the Alberta Legislature and as the provincial minister of Education. Boyle was appointed to the Supreme Court of Alberta. Boyle is 35 km southeast of Athabasca.

BRACHIOPOD MOUNTAIN (2530 m) This mountain is named after the brachiopod and coral fossils found on its west slope. Brachiopod Mountain is 45 km northwest of Banff.

BRAGG CREEK Pop. 651. In 1911, this hamlet was named after Albert W. Bragg, the earliest settler in the area. Bragg Creek is approximately 30 km west of Calgary.

BRANT This hamlet took its name from the Brant species of geese, plentiful in the vicinity when the community was founded in 1905. Brant is 63 km southeast of Calgary.

BRAZEAU RANGE This range near Nordegg was named after Joseph E. Brazeau. He worked for the Hudson's Bay Company in Edmonton, Rocky Mountain House and Jasper House from 1852 to 1864. In addition to speaking French, Spanish and English, Brazeau spoke several Native languages. With his facility for languages, he assisted members of the Palliser Expedition as a translator. (see Palliser Pass)

BREAKER MOUNTAIN (3058 m) The name for this mountain refers to wave-like snow formations found on its slopes. It is about 100 km northwest of Banff.

B

BRETON Pop. 521. This village is 36 km southeast of Drayton Valley and was named after Douglas Corney Breton (1883–1953). Breton served in the United Farmers of Alberta provincial government from 1926 to 1930. The post office was previously known as Keystone.

BROCKET Pop. 1537. This hamlet near Pincher Creek was named after Brocket Hall, the seat of Baron Mount Stephen, in Hatfield, Herts, England. George Stephen (1829–1921) was a director of the Bank of Montreal and of the CPR.

BROOKS Pop. 13,000. This city 100 km northwest of Medicine Hat took its name from Noell Edgell Brooks. He was a CPR divisional engineer from 1903 to 1913. The first post office opened here in 1904. Brooks became a village in 1910, a town one year later and finally a city in 2005. In 1914, the Brooks Aqueduct began delivering irrigation water to southeast Alberta. When it was built, the 3.2-km-long aqueduct was the longest steel-reinforced concrete structure of its kind in the world. The Brooks Aqueduct, built by the Canadian Pacific Railway, was in operation for 65 years and is now a national and provincial historic site.

BROSSEAU A post office was opened in this hamlet in 1904 and was named after its first postmaster, Edmond Brosseau, a successful merchant and farmer. Before coming to the area, Brosseau served in the Union Army during the U.S. Civil War. (see St. Paul)

BROWNFIELD This hamlet 26 km north of Coronation was named after Charles Dee Brownfield, a well-known local rancher and the first postmaster of the community. In the early 1900s, C.D. Brownfield promoted cattle-brand inspection among ranchers.

BROWNVALE This hamlet near Grimshaw was named after an early homesteader in the area, John Brown.

B

BRUCE This hamlet near Viking once had the name Hurry. Apparently officials in Ottawa did not like the name, so it was changed in 1909 to Bruce, after A. Bruce Smith, manager of the Grand Trunk Pacific Telegraph Company.

BRUDERHEIM Pop. 1198. The town of Bruderheim was originally a Moravian settlement. Its name is German for "brethren home." In 1893, Andreas Lilge came to Canada to find a new home for some members of the Moravian Church who had migrated from Poland to Russia. Lilge found this location near Edmonton and was joined by his two brothers, William and Ludwig, and other settlers from the "Old Country." In honour of the three brothers, the community was named Bruderheim.

BRUSSELS PEAK (3161 m) This mountain peak was named after the ship captained by Charles Algernon Fryatt (1872–1916). Fryatt was a World War I merchant seaman hero. Brussels Peak is 44 km southeast of Jasper. Mount Fryatt was also named after C.A. Fryatt.

BUCK LAKE This hamlet took its name from the nearby lake. In Cree the lake is called *ya-pe-oo*, meaning "bull moose." Buck Lake is 80 km west of Wetaskiwin.

BUFFALO It is not certain how this hamlet 85 km north of Medicine Hat received its name. The most likely explanation is that a local resident, Mr. Pauling, who had come from Buffalo, New York, was instrumental in naming this community after the U.S. city. Other people suggest the name came from the buffalo that roamed the area. The community was started in 1914 with the building of a Canadian Pacific Railway station.

BUFFALO LAKE This lake near Bashaw took its name from its Cree name *Mustus*. The Cree name refers to the outline of the lake, which resembles the outline of a stretched buffalo skin.

B

BUFORD This hamlet near Edmonton got its name from a town in North Dakota. The post office operated here for 66 years, opening in 1903 and closing in 1969.

BURDETT Pop. 286. This village was named after Angela Georgina, Baroness Burdett-Coutts (1814–1906). She was left a fortune by her step-grandmother, the Duchess of St. Albans. The baroness used part of her wealth to invest in coal mining in southern Alberta, and she was a shareholder in the North West Coal and Navigation Company and the Alberta Railway and Irrigation Company. (see Coutts)

BUSBY Pop. 73. It is believed this hamlet was named after Edward Busby, the inspector of customs in the Yukon during the Klondike Gold Rush. Before 1915 its post office was named Independence.

BUTTE This locality took its name from a hill, or butte, in the area. The mound, which Native legend says was made by the Great Spirit, resembles a kneeling buffalo. Area Natives took this "kneeling buffalo" butte as a sign the animal would be plentiful for their food and clothing.

BUTTRESS MOUNTAIN (2685 m) This mountain is so named because the cliffs that surround it form a buttress. Buttress Mountain is about 24 km south of Jasper.

BYEMOOR Pop. 39. This hamlet was named by Leonard Browne after his hometown in England. Its post office opened under that name in 1925. Byemoor is about 44 km northwest of Hanna.

C

CADOGAN This hamlet near Provost was likely named after George Henry, the Fifth Earl of Cadogan, under-secretary of State for the Colonies in the late 1800s and lord lieutenant of Ireland.

CADOMIN Pop. 86. The name for this hamlet is a contraction of "Canadian Dominion Mine." It was a suggestion of F.L. Hammond, first president of the Cadomin Coal Company. The community was established in 1913.

CADOTTE LAKE Pop. 316. The hamlet took its name from fur trader Jean Baptiste Cadotte (1723–1803). In the late 1700s, Cadotte expanded his business and became part of a larger group of traders including Peter Pond and Thomas Frobisher. Nearby Cadotte River was recorded as Cadotte's River in an explorer's journal in 1828. Cadotte Lake is about 57 km northeast of Peace River.

CAIRN HILL This site, about 87 km east of Lethbridge, was named for the Native cairn atop this hill. A cairn is a heap of stones piled up as a memorial or landmark.

CAIRNGORM (2610 m) This mountain took its name from the Cairngorm Mountains in Scotland. Cairngorm is near Jasper.

CALAHOO Pop. 126. This hamlet was named after William Calahoo, a Métis who was employed with the fur companies. The community is approximately 35 km northwest of Edmonton.

CALAIS This hamlet on the Sturgeon Lake Indian Reserve is named for Reverend Jules Marie Calais (1871–1944), an Oblate missionary. Father Calais was the second priest in charge of the old mission on Sturgeon Lake. Calais is near Valleyview.

C

CALGARY Pop. 1,060,000 (metropolitan area). With the Rockies as its panoramic backdrop, this city, steeped in frontier history, took its name from the ancestral estate of Lieutenant-Colonel James Farquharson Macleod of the North-West Mounted Police. Lieutenant-Colonel Macleod's ancestral estate was on the Isle of Mull in the Hebrides in Scotland. As part of the "Great March of 1874" to western Canada to stop the illicit whiskey trade, Lieutenant-Colonel Macleod set up headquarters at a small post named in his honour. This was Fort Macleod, now a town. Inspector A. Brisebois and 50 men left Fort Macleod to establish another post, located where the Elbow River flows into the Bow River. This is how Calgary got its start. Inspector Brisebois wanted to call the new post after himself, but he was overruled by Macleod (by then promoted to assistant commissioner) who decided that the name would be Calgary. In 1876, the federal government officially approved the name. There are different views on the origin and meaning of "Calgary." Some suggest it is Gaelic for "clear running water," but others say it is Gaelic for a "bay farm." The Blackfoot name for the site of today's city of Calgary was *moll-inistsis-in-aka-apewis*, and the Cree name was *o-toos-kwa-nik*. Both refer to the Elbow River.

Calgary, at first only a North-West Mounted Police post, became a prominent trading post. Since then, the city has evolved into a major financial centre in Canada, a leader in the oil and natural gas industry and the centre of a large cattle business. It is known worldwide for "the Greatest Outdoor Show on Earth"—the Calgary Exhibition and Stampede, held every summer.

CALLING LAKE The long-standing Native name for this lake northwest of Lac La Biche referred to the loud noises the lake makes when it freezes over each year.

C

CALMAR Pop. 1797. The first postmaster of this community, C.J. Blomquist, chose the name after his hometown of Kalmar, Sweden. This town is 42 km southwest of Edmonton.

CALUMET PEAK (2977 m) This peak 86 km northwest of Jasper took its name from the nearby fort Pierre au Calumet. *Calumet* is Cree for "peace pipe," so the fort's name translates as "Pierre with peace pipe."

CAMERON FALLS, CAMERON LAKE and CAMERON MOUNTAIN These features near the hamlet of Waterton Park are named after Captain Donald Roderick Cameron (1834–1921). He was the British Commissioner on the International Boundary Commission of 1872–76. Cameron Mountain (2565 m), a part of Buchanan Ridge, was previously known as Cameronian Mountain.

CAMPSIE This former hamlet was named in 1909 after Campsie, Strathclyde, Scotland. It comes from the Gaelic *cam sith,* meaning "crooked hill."

CAMROSE Pop. 15,850. The name for this city was picked from the British postal guide in 1905 and refers to Camrose, Dyfed, Wales. How Camrose, Wales, got its name is uncertain. The name, already in Anglicized form, first appears in 1324 as *kamros,* meaning "crooked moor," said to come from the Welsh *cam rhos.* On the other hand, perhaps the name comes from *cwm rose,* meaning "valley of the roses," using the Welsh word *cwn* (valley). Camrose, primarily an agricultural community, is 70 km southeast of Edmonton

MORE ABOUT CAMROSE...*During the first weekend of August, Camrose hosts the Big Valley Jamboree. With top country-music entertainers and superstars, it is the third largest country music show in North America. It usually draws about 60,000 fans.*

C

CANADIAN FORCES BASE COLD LAKE This military base is located near the town of Cold Lake. (see Cold Lake)

CANICHE PEAK (2552 m) This mountain peak near Jasper resembles the shape of a poodle's head. *Caniche* is the French word for "poodle."

CANMORE Pop. 10,239. In 1884, the first divisional point west of Calgary was established, and it seems CPR executive Donald Smith, later Lord Strathcona, named the railway centre after the nickname for the Scottish king Malcolm III. Malcolm III's nickname derived from the Gaelic *ceann mor,* meaning "big head." He reigned from 1057 to 1093 after defeating MacBeth, another aspirant to the throne. Canmore is a town located southeast of Banff.

CAPRICORN GLACIER This glacier, about 100 km northwest of Banff, was named for the mountain goats in the area. *Capricorn* is Latin for "goat."

CARBON Pop. 450. This village took its name from the coal mines in the area. Carbon is also a ranching and farming centre. It originally was known as the Kneehill Post Office.

CARBONDALE Pop. 75. This hamlet near Edmonton was named for the coal deposits in the district.

CARDIFF The name of this former hamlet near Edmonton reflects the coal-mining activity in the area and also refers to the Welsh mining centre of Cardiff.

CARDSTON Pop. 3417. This town was named after Charles Ora Card, son-in-law of Mormon leader Brigham Young. In 1866, Card came from Utah to set up a new home in southern Alberta for members of the Church of Jesus Christ of Latter-day Saints (Mormons). The following year, 10 families joined Card and took up squatters' rights near Lees Creek, on the present site of Cardston. This community, about 65 km southwest of Lethbridge, became a town in 1901.

CARIBOU MOUNTAINS (height unknown) It is likely the name of these mountains refers to the large number of caribou found in the area. The Caribou Mountains are about 97 km northeast of High Level.

CARMANGAY Pop. 258. This village north of Lethbridge was named for Charles Carman and his wife Gertrude, née Gay, early residents of the area. A combination of their surnames gave the village its name.

CAROLINE Pop. 472. This village took its name from the only child of Mr. and Mrs. Harvey Langley, who opened the first post office in 1908. The village of Caroline is the boyhood home of Kurt Browning, four-time world champion in figure skating. Caroline is 34 km southeast of Rocky Mountain House.

CARSELAND Pop. 652. *Carse* is Scottish for "fertile land." The hamlet, located near Calgary, was named for its particularly rich river valley land.

CARSTAIRS Pop. 2086. This town was named after Carstairs, Lanarkshire, Scotland. Carstairs is about 82 km south-southwest of Red Deer.

CARUSO This former village 35 km east of Calgary was originally named Cheadle but took the name of Caruso in 1917. Caruso (1873–1921) was the world-acclaimed Italian tenor who gained fame for his operatic performances. The reason for the locality's change of name is not known.

CARVEL American author Winston Churchill (not the British statesman, Winston Spencer Churchill) wrote a popular romance novel, *Richard Carvel*. This hamlet near Stony Plain took its name from the novel.

C

CASCADE MOUNTAIN (2998 m) This mountain was named in 1858 by Sir James Hector of the Palliser Expedition. The name is derived from its Native name, translated as "Mountain Where the Water Falls." Cascade Mountain overlooks the town of Banff.

CASKET MOUNTAIN (2231 m) Near the summit of this mountain is a formation that resembles a casket. Casket Mountain is 55 km southwest of Grande Cache.

CASSILS This former hamlet was named for Charles Cassils of the Montréal firm of Cassils, Cochrane and Co. Cassils and his partner Matthew Cochrane were involved in the Cochrane Ranch. The hamlet is about 112 km northeast of Lethbridge.

CASTELETS, THE (2877 m/2744 m) This mountain's two peaks resemble small castles. The Castelets is located about 110 km southeast of Jasper.

CASTLE ISLAND Pop. 19. This summer village is on an island in Lac Ste. Anne. The island was once owned by Frenchman Count de Caze, who had a dream of building a stone castle on it. De Caze died before his castle was completed. At one time, the island was known as Constance Island.

CASTLE MOUNTAIN (2862 m) This mountain near Banff was named by Sir James Hector of the 1857–60 Palliser Expedition after its shape. In 1946, the mountain was renamed Mount Eisenhower to honour General Dwight D. Eisenhower, who had commanded the Allied forces in Europe during World War II. Under public pressure the name reverted in 1979 to its original name.(see Eisenhower Peak)

C

CASTLEGUARD MOUNTAIN (3090 m) This mountain took its name from its castle-like appearance and its position as majestic guardian over the southern portion of the Columbia Icefield. Castleguard Mountain is about 100 km southeast of Jasper.

CASTOR Pop. 970. *Castor* is Latin for "beaver." This town got its name from the large number of beaver in the vicinity and its proximity to Beaverdam Creek, which runs through the community. Castor is 140 km east of Red Deer.

CATACOMBS MOUNTAIN (3330 m) This mountain 55 km southeast of Jasper has an alcove-like overhang that has been likened to the underground burial tombs of the early Christians in Rome.

CATARACT PEAK (3333 m) This mountain peak 65 km northwest of Banff was named after a waterfall in the area.

CAUDRON PEAK (2547 m) The origin of this mountain's name is not certain. It is near Bellevue.

CAVE MOUNTAIN (2651 m) It is believed this mountain was so named because it contains a cave. Cave Mountain is about 100 km west of Calgary.

CAVENDISH This former village north of Medicine Hat was named in 1917 for Victor Christian William Cavendish, the Duke of Devonshire. He served as governor general from 1916 to 1921. This locality was previously known as Pancras, after a borough of London, England.

CAYLEY This hamlet 55 km south of Calgary was named for Hugh St. Quentin Cayley (1857–1934). He was owner/editor of the *Calgary Herald* in the late 1880s. He also served on the Legislative Council and the Legislative Assembly of the North-West Territories.

C

CENTRE PEAK (2547 m) This mountain near Bellevue is so named because it is centred between the heads of two valleys.

CEREAL Pop. 198. This village took its name from the area's reputation for producing large yields of various grains. Cereal is about 138 km east of Drumheller.

CESSFORD In an effort to remember their home in Sweden, homesteaders Axel Anderson and his wife chose the name Cess Fiord, or Cessford, for this hamlet. It is about 94 km southeast of Drumheller.

CHABA PEAK (3212 m) This mountain was named after Stoney Native Joe Beaver. *Chaba* is the Stoney word for "beaver." Chaba Peak is about 80 km southeast of Jasper.

CHAK PEAK (2774 m) The name of this mountain near Jasper is a Native word for "eagle."

CHAMPION Pop. 362. This village and railway stop was named after H.T. Champion of the Winnipeg banking firm Alloway and Champion. Originally known as Cleverville after an early settler in the district, Champion is about 65 km northwest of Lethbridge.

CHANCELLOR Pop. 16. This hamlet was named in 1913 after Theobald von Bethman-Holleg, the chancellor of Germany at the time. This hamlet, inhabited mainly by settlers of German heritage, suffered an extensive fire in the 1930s and never bounced back. It is located 85 km east of Calgary.

CHATEH This post office was named in honour of Chief Chateh, who signed Treaty 8 in 1900. Chateh, formerly known as Assumption, is located northwest of High Level in northern Alberta. (see Assumption)

CHAUVIN Pop. 400. This village was named after George von Chauvin, a director of the Grand Truck Pacific

Railway. Chauvin's post office opened in 1909. The community is about 38 km north of Provost.

CHEADLE Pop. 66. This hamlet near Calgary was named after Dr. Walter Cheadle (1835–1910). Dr. Cheadle, an explorer, co-authored *The Northwest Passage by Land*. From 1862 to 1863, Cheadle and Viscount Milton crossed the Prairies and the Rocky Mountains to reach the Pacific Coast.

CHERHILL This hamlet was named in 1911 after part of the name of the area's first postmaster, A.P. Stecher. "Hill" was added to "cher" to form the full name of the community.

CHESTERMERE LAKE There are different theories about how this lake near Calgary was named. Some claim it was named for Lord Chester, a senior executive with the Canadian Pacific Railway. Others contend it was named after Lord Chestermere.

CHETAMON MOUNTAIN (2504 m) Two rocks on this mountain have the appearance of a squirrel. *Chetamon* is the Stoney word for "squirrel." Chetamon Mountain is near Jasper.

CHEVIOT MOUNTAIN (2720 m) This mountain was named after the Cheviot Hills in England. It was named by H.M. Thornton of the Mountain Park Coal Company, who thought the shape of the mountain resembled the hills in his former homeland. Cheviot Mountain is about 50 km east of Jasper.

CHEVRON MOUNTAIN (2853 m) This is a descriptive name for this mountain about 26 km south of Jasper. The chevron name refers to inverted "V"s.

CHIN Pop. 23. This locality east of Lethbridge took its name from a nearby hill, Chin Butte, that when viewed from a distance resembles a chin. The Blackfoot refer to the hill as *mistoamo*, meaning "beard."

C

CHINOOK PEAK (2591 m) This mountain took its name from local residents who say that before a chinook occurs, peculiar winds and clouds gather on the east side of the peak. Chinook Peak is near Coleman.

CHINOOK This hamlet about 150 km north of Medicine Hat was named after the warm, dry winds that sometimes blow across the Rocky Mountains from the Pacific Ocean.

MORE ABOUT CHINOOK... *Taking its name from the Chinook Natives who lived in Oregon, a chinook wind can cause temperatures to rise dramatically during winter months. In recorded cases, temperatures have gone up 20°C in an hour. During a chinook, warm, gusty winds replace an Arctic air mass with warm Pacific air and quickly turn winter into spring for a few hours or even a few days. As the Pacific air mass crosses the Rocky Mountains, it loses its moisture and descends on the eastern side of the mountains as a dry wind. When a chinook appears, a bright arch appears across the sky, locally referred to as a chinook arch. Although chinooks do occur in the northern parts of the province, they are more often experienced in the southwest area of Alberta. According to legend, Chinook, a beautiful Native maiden, was lost in the mountains, and when a soft gentle wind came from the west, her loved ones supposed it was a reminder of her presence.*

CHIPMAN Pop. 230. A Canadian Northern Railway station and post office were opened here in 1905. The hamlet, about 58 km northeast of Edmonton, was named after C.C. Chipman (1856–1924). He was private secretary to Sir Charles Tupper, who was minister of Railways and Canals in the Conservative government in 1882. Chipman was later named chief commissioner of the Hudson's Bay Company.

CHISHOLM Pop. 25. This hamlet was named after Thomas Chisholm, a Klondike pioneer and railway contractor. The hamlet of Chisholm was first established as an Edmonton, Dunvegan and British Columbia Railway station in 1914. Chisholm is 60 km southwest of Athabasca.

CINQUEFOIL MOUNTAIN (2259 m) This mountain 50 km southwest of Hinton was named after the cinquefoil that grows in the area. The cinquefoil, commonly called potentilla, is a small shrub related to the rose.

CIRQUE PEAK (2993 m) This descriptive name made note of the shape of the mountain's limestone formations that give the impression of a cirque or amphitheatre. Cirque Peak is 85 km northwest of Banff.

CITADEL PEAK (2610 m) The fortress-like shape of this mountain gave it its name. Citadel Peak is near Banff.

CLANDONALD Pop. 146. This hamlet near Vermilion took its name from the prominent Scottish clan Donald. The post office opened here in 1927. Clandonald was formerly known as Wellsdale.

CLARESHOLM Pop. 3427. This agricultural town 64 km northwest of Lethbridge was named by John Niblock. The Canadian Pacific Railway superintendent named the small railway centre in 1891 after the name of his home in Medicine Hat. His wife's name was Clare, so he called their home "Clare's Home." Claresholm's incorporation as a town on August 31, 1905 was among the last legislation passed by the North-West Territorial government. The next day, Alberta became a province.

CLAYSMORE It is believed this locality near Edmonton was named after a village in Middlesex, now part of Greater London.

C

CLEARWATER MOUNTAIN (3275 m) This mountain took its name from the nearby Clearwater River. Clearwater Mountain is 75 km northwest of Banff.

CLEARWATER RIVER This name is derived from its Native name *wa-se-ka-mew-see pee*, meaning "clear water." This river is the largest tributary of the Athabasca River. Fur trader Peter Pond travelled the Clearwater River in 1778.

CLIFF MOUNTAIN (2743 m) This is a descriptive name for the steep cliffs along the face of this mountain near Jasper.

CLIMAX MOUNTAIN (2823 m) This descriptive name refers to the mountain's summit, which reaches high above a long ridge. Climax Mountain is 44 km east of Jasper.

CLIVE Pop. 517. This village was named for Robert Clive (1725–74), who established British rule in India. The village, incorporated in 1909, is near Lacombe. Clive was previously known as Valley City.

CLOISTER MOUNTAINS (height unknown) These mountains 115 km southeast of Jasper resemble four cathedrals. Nearby Minister Mountain parallels the religious theme.

CLOVER BAR This bar in the North Saskatchewan River (previously known as Clover's Bar) took its name from Thomas H. Clover (1829–97?). He was a wanderer and a participant in California's 1849 gold rush. Clover was then in the Cariboo (BC) Gold Rush and later moved to Edmonton, where he panned for gold on the North Saskatchewan River. Eventually, Clover moved to North Dakota. A locality located both inside and outside Edmonton's present-day east boundary, a school district and a post office took the name Clover Bar around 1890.

CLUNY This hamlet was named after Cluny Parish in Aberdeenshire, Scotland. Cluny is about 75 km east of Calgary.

CLYDE Pop. 427. This village near Westlock was named after George Clyde, a homesteader in the area. He was its first postmaster, and his home, stocked with many essentials, was a stopping place for area residents and travellers.

COALDALE Pop. 5731. At first only a railway siding, Coaldale, now a town, took its name from the name of the nearby residence of coal mine-owner Elliott Galt. Mr. Galt's residence had been named Coaldale, while two other nearby communities also had coal-related names: Coalbanks and Coalhurst. Coaldale is located 10 km east of Lethbridge.

COALHURST Pop. 1465. The name of this village near Lethbridge refers to the abundance of coal in the area and is the surname of an early settler in the area, Mr. Hurst. Coalhurst and Coalbanks were names in common usage for the area, and in 1885 they were given one name, Lethbridge. However, in 1979, Coalhurst re-emerged as a village separate from Lethbridge.

COCKSCOMB MOUNTAIN (2776 m) This is a descriptive name for this mountain near Banff that resembles the comb of a cock.

COCHRANE Pop. 10,391. This town was named after Québec Senator Matthew Cochrane (1823–1903) who owned the Cochrane Ranch. The ranch was established in 1881 and was the first major ranching company in western Canada. Cochrane is the home of the Western Heritage Centre, which gives a comprehensive overview and history of the western cattle industry. Cochrane is about 22 km northwest of Calgary.

C

COLD LAKE This is a descriptive name for the waters of the lake, which remain cold in all seasons. Cold Lake is about 133 km north of Lloydminster. The city of Cold Lake, with a population of 11,595, was formed in 2000, by the amalgamation of the town of Cold Lake, Grand Centre and the civilian areas of Canadian Forces Base Cold Lake.

COLEMAN Pop. 6500. This former town took its name from Florence Coleman Flumerfelt, the daughter of A.C. Flumerfelt, president of the International Coal and Coke Company. Coleman is near Blairmore, in the Crowsnest Pass. In 1979, Coleman was consolidated with other communities in the Crowsnest Pass to form the Municipality of Crowsnest Pass. (see Crowsnest Pass)

COLINTON This hamlet near Athabasca was named in 1912 after the townsite of Colinton, Edinburgh, Scotland. It was named by J.M. Milne, an early settler in the area. Before 1912, Colinton, Alberta was known as Kinnoull.

COLISEUM MOUNTAIN (1981 m) This mountain near Nordegg resembles a round coliseum.

COLLEGE HEIGHTS Pop. 272. This hamlet near Lacombe took this name because it contained a Seventh-Day Adventist school located on a hill.

COLUMBIA ICEFIELD This icefield, about 95 km southeast of Jasper, contains the largest amount of ice in the Rockies. The icefield covers some 337 square kilometres. Its runoff flows into three major rivers: the Athabasca, flowing north to the Arctic Ocean; the Saskatchewan, flowing east to Hudson Bay; and the Columbia, flowing west to the Pacific. (see Mount Columbia)

COMMITTEE PUNCH BOWL This circular basin at the summit of Athabasca Pass, 55 km south of Jasper, was a common meeting place for Hudson's Bay Company factors who were said to be the Governing Committee of the Hudson's Bay Company.

COMMONWEALTH PEAK (2774 m) This peak, about 85 km west-southwest of Calgary, was named after the XI Commonwealth Games held in Edmonton in 1978.

COMPEER It is said the early settlers of this hamlet felt equal, hence the name Compeer. Previously known as Sleepy Hollow, Compeer is 57 km southeast of Provost.

CONDOR This hamlet was named after the gunboat HMS *Condor*, commanded by Captain Lord Charles Beresford. The *Condor* bombarded Alexandria, Egypt, in 1882. Condor is about 53 km northwest of Red Deer.

CONE MOUNTAIN (2896 m) This name is descriptive of the cone-shaped mountain. Cone Mountain is about 90 km west of Calgary.

CONKLIN Pop. 145. This hamlet, about 110 km northeast of Lac La Biche, was named after John Conklin. He was a timekeeper for railway contractor J.D. McArthur. The post office opened in Conklin in 1924.

CONRICH The name of this hamlet is taken from the surnames of two real estate promoters, Connacher and Richardson. Conrich is near Calgary.

CONSORT Pop. 794. This village southwest of Provost was named in honour of the coronation of King George V and his consort Queen Mary in 1911. This community was previously called the Sanderville Post Office. Consort was the girlhood home of international recording star k.d. lang.

MORE ABOUT CONSORT...*It is a good thing for the music and entertainment world that Kathryn Dawn Lang (k.d. lang) did not take to heart discouraging words about her image and music*

C

when starting out in the early 1980s in central Alberta. k.d., with her chopped off cowboy boots, funky clothes and country punk music, persisted and is now seen as a transcendent artist, always knocking at the conventions of music. k.d. lang did not take her exceptional voice for granted and worked hard on and off the music circuit polishing her talent. She listened to other bands and singers and later said she considered the diverse music played on public radio CKUA in Edmonton an important part of her musical development. Her first single record with her band The Reclines was Friday Dance Promenade. Many albums have followed including Absolute Torch and Twang (1989), which earned her a well-deserved Grammy for Best Female Country Vocalist. Starting the millennium with a new album, Invincible Summer, k.d. is now in a more contemplative, breezy musical mode, showing a diversity that hints at the immense talent of this international star.

COOKING LAKE It is believed this area was a favourite Native camping ground, and the name for the locality is a translation of the Cree word *opi mi now wa sioo*. Cooking Lake is east of Edmonton.

COPPER MOUNTAIN (2795 m) This mountain near Banff took its name from copper found near its summit.

CORNWALL CREEK This creek east of Grande Prairie is likely named after legendary James "Peace River Jim" Cornwall.

MORE ABOUT JAMES CORNWALL… *James "Peace River Jim" Cornwall (1871–1955) was born in Ontario and arrived in Athabasca Landing in 1896. Cornwall started various businesses in the area and sat as Liberal MLA for Peace River from 1908 to 1912. "Peace River Jim," served as a lieutenant colonel in the Canadian Expeditionary Force during World War I and was decorated for his efforts by King George V and the French government. After the war* *he returned to the Peace River area. He died in Calgary in 1955 at the age of 84.*

C

CORONACH MOUNTAIN (2462 m) This mountain was named after howling coyotes, the sound of which resembles a funeral cry. *Coranach* is Gaelic for "a funeral dirge." Coronach Mountain is 40 km north of Jasper.

CORONATION Pop. 1166. This town was named in honour of the coronation in 1911 of King George V. Some of the streets and avenues also recognize the royal event, taking names like George, King, Queen, Victoria and Mary.

CORONATION MOUNTAIN (3170 m) This mountain was named to commemorate the coronation on August 9, 1901 of King Edward VII and Queen Alexandra. Coronation Mountain is about 40 km north of Jasper.

CORONET MOUNTAIN (3152 m) This descriptive name refers to the crown-like shape of this mountain. Coronet Mountain is about 89 km west of Nordegg.

COUGAR MOUNTAIN (2863 m) This mountain about 43 km west of Turner Valley was so named because cougars were sighted in the area.

COUTTS Pop. 386. There are different theories for how this village was named. Perhaps it was named after Sir William Lehman A. Burdett-Coutts (née Bartlett). He was a banker, a member of the British Parliament in the late 1800s and a director of the Alberta Railway and Irrigation Company. Another version claims Coutts was named after Sir William's wife, Angela Georgina, Baroness Burdett-Coutts (1814–1906). Her step-grandmother, the Duchess of St. Albans, left her a fortune, and she was once described as "the richest heiress in England." She invested in the Alberta Railway and Irrigation Company and the North West Coal and Navigation Company. Baroness

Burdett-Coutts is buried in Westminster Abbey. Coutts is 95 km southeast of Lethbridge. (see Burdett)

C

COWLEY Pop. 273. There are differing accounts of how this village near Pincher Creek was named. Perhaps it was named by local rancher F.W. Godsal after his hometown in England. Another possibility also involves Godsal and suggests that, while watching his cattle graze, he was reminded of a line from Gray's "Elegy Written in a Country Courtyard": "...the lowing herd winds slowly o'er the lea." *Lea* or *ley* is the Anglo-Saxon word for "pasture," so when asked to name the community, Godsal put "cow" and "ley" together to form "Cowley."

CRAIGMYLE This hamlet close to Hanna was named after an estate in Scotland. The word *craig* is Gaelic for "rock."

CREMONA Pop. 380. This picturesque village nestled in the foothills was named after an Italian city famous for its violins. Cremona is 28 km west of Carstairs.

CROSS CREEK This creek was named after Alfred E. Cross (1861–1932). He was an early rancher in the Calgary area. He also set up Calgary Brewing and Malting Company in the late 1800s. Cross was one of the first to assist in financing the Calgary Stampede.

MORE ABOUT CROSS CREEK...*A young Alfred E. Cross arrived in Calgary in 1884. A graduate of eastern veterinary and agricultural schools, Cross worked at Senator Cochrane's ranch before striking out on his own. In 1888, a riding accident determined that Cross would have to leave the wide open spaces of the country and live in Calgary where he had better access to medical treatment. The resilient Cross hit upon the idea of brewing beer for thirsty westerners. His Calgary Brewing and Malting Company was a success, and Cross prospered. By 1912, he owned one of the largest ranches in the province and helped develop several other major* companies—*Alberta Flour Mills, Royalite Oil and Canadian Western Natural Gas. Cross also served as an elected member of the Legislative Assembly for the North-West Territories where he promoted provincial status for Alberta. Perhaps Cross is best remembered as one of the "Big Four" who put up money to start the Calgary Exhibition and Stampede, a fitting tribute to a person who always remained a rancher at heart.*

CROSSFIELD Pop. 2003. Named after a railway engineer, this town is located 45 km north of Calgary.

CROWFOOT This former locality 110 km southeast of Calgary was named after Chief Crowfoot (ca. 1836–90).

MORE ABOUT CROWFOOT...*Considered by many as a chief among chiefs for his vision, diplomacy, leadership and courage, Crowfoot, head of the Blackfoot Confederacy, played an important part in shaping the Prairies. Crowfoot made peace with the Cree, supported the North-West Mounted Police in ending the illegal whisky trade and refused to take part in the 1885 Riel Rebellion—a fight he thought would be futile for his people. In 1887, Crowfoot had a prominent role in negotiating and signing Treaty 7, which set aside reserves for the Blood, Blackfoot and Peigan. Poor health was with Crowfoot in the last years of his life, and he died in the Siksika (Blackfoot) Indian Reserve in 1890.*

CROWFOOT CREEK This creek about 110 km southeast of Calgary flows southwest into the Bow River. It was named after Chief Crowfoot. (see Crowfoot)

CROWFOOT MOUNTAIN (3050 m) This descriptive name refers to a glacier on the mountain that resembles a crow's foot. Crowfoot Mountain is about 80 km northwest of Banff.

C

CROWSNEST MOUNTAIN (2785 m) The mountain's name comes from the Cree name *kak-ka-ioo-wut-tshis-tun*. It means "the nest of the crow or raven." The name goes back to 1858 when Captain Blakiston of the Palliser Expedition first noted it in his records. Crowsnest Mountain is about 52 km northwest of Pincher Creek.

CROWSNEST PASS (1246 m) This pass is about 55 km northwest of Pincher Creek. (see Crowsnest Mountain)

CROWSNEST PASS, MUNICIPALITY OF Pop. 6356. In 1979, several communities along Highway 3 in the Crows-nest Pass were consolidated. The towns of Blairmore and Coleman; the villages of Bellevue, Frank and Hillcrest Mines; and other hamlets in the Pass came together under one municipal government following passage of the Crows-nest Pass Municipal Unification Act. Although the names of the original towns and villages are still in use, residents in the communities and surrounding area now elect nine aldermen and a mayor to govern their municipality as a whole.

CURATOR MOUNTAIN (2622 m) This mountain took its name from its so-called position as custodian of Shovel Pass. The pass is part of a route to the Maligne Valley. Curator Mountain is near Jasper.

CURIA MOUNTAIN (2835 m) The descriptive name for this mountain refers to the fact it looks like a Roman senate house, or curia. Curia Mountain is near Jasper.

CUTBANK RIVER Cutbank River took its name from its steep banks that rise 150 metres in places. Cutbank River is about 50 km southeast of Grande Prairie.

CYCLONE MOUNTAIN (3050 m) This mountain was named after a storm on its peak. Cyclone Mountain is about 55 km northwest of Banff.

CYNTHIA This hamlet near Drayton Valley was named after the daughter of the first hotelkeeper in the community.

CYPRESS HILLS These hills located in southeastern Alberta and southwestern Saskatchewan take their name from their French name *les montanes des Cyprès*. They got this name when some westward-bound Red River Métis equated the area's trees with the jack-pines *(le cyprè)* they had known in Manitoba. *Les Montanes des Cyprès* was anglicized by English settlers to "Cypress Hills." The hills cover about 2500 square kilometres and were known by the Cree as *mi-na-ti-kak,* meaning "beautiful upland."

CYPRESS HILLS PROVINCIAL PARK With a few minor boundary changes, this provincial park contains the 490-square-kilometre protected area set aside in 1911 under federal legislation. Some 207 square kilometres of this area are in Alberta with the remaining portion in Saskatchewan. In 1930, the federal government gave the Alberta government control of the Alberta portion, which was known as the Elkwater Block. (see Elkwater) (see Cypress Hills)

CZAR Pop. 199. The origin of this place name is not clear. Some suggest that Russian workers on a nearby section of the Canadian Pacific Railway chose the name. Others say the village was named to commemorate the signing in 1907 of the Anglo-Russian Treaty. There is also an account that the name was a reference to the boss *(czar)* on a railway crew. Czar is about 40 km northwest of Provost.

D

DAIS MOUNTAIN (3300 m) The descriptive name for this mountain refers to the way it is raised as a platform. Dais Mountain is about 75 km southeast of Jasper.

DALEMEAD This hamlet took its name from its location in a dale or valley and from the name of irrigation specialist Dr. Ellwood Mead. Another account states the community was first known as Needmore, but a school and then a railway point took the name Strathmead. The local branch of the UFA expressed concern Strathmead would be confused with the nearby town of Strathmore so changed the first part to "dale."

DALROY This locality near Calgary took its name from the Scottish prefix *dale*, meaning "valley" and the name of early settler G.M. McElroy.

DAPP Pop. 29. This hamlet near Westlock forms its name from the initials of railway worker David A. Pennicuick. "D.A.P." and an extra "p" spells the name of this community. Dapp was previously known as Eunice.

DARWELL This hamlet was named for the biblical character Darwall. It is not known why the spelling was changed. Darwell is approximately 33 km northwest of Stony Plain.

DAYSLAND Pop. 679. This town bears the name of Egerton W. Day, the first settler in the area. Daysland, southeast of Camrose, was incorporated as a town in 1907, and Day was its first mayor.

DE WINTON This hamlet was named in honour of Major-General Sir Francis De Winton, G.C.M.G., C.B. De Winton (1835–1901) was military secretary to the

Marquess of Lorne, governor general from 1878 to 1883. He also organized the De Winton Ranch Co. (known by some as the Brecon Ranch). De Winton is on the southern outskirts of Calgary.

DEAD MAN FLAT This flat is about 8 km southeast of Canmore. There are different stories about why this name is used. One involves François Marrett, who supposedly killed his brother John with an axe. Another story tells of two Natives who were trapping beaver. It is not clear why they wanted to avoid questioning by an approaching park warden, but they did so by covering themselves with beaver blood and playing dead. When the warden went for assistance, the two got up and took their pelts home.

DEAD MAN'S FLATS This locality east of Canmore was named for its proximity to Dead Man Flat.

DEAD MANS PASS This pass located near Coleman got its name when a group of Natives ambushed about 40 U.S. cavalrymen there. According to legend, the Natives killed all the soldiers.

DEADLODGE CANYON This canyon about 94 km northwest of Medicine Hat took its name from the Blackfoot name *eh-taka-skeeneema*, meaning "where there are many of our dead lodges." It refers to a time smallpox killed many Natives in the area.

DEBOLT Pop. 116. This hamlet approximately 50 km eastnortheast of Grande Prairie was named after H.E. DeBolt (1888–1969). He served as the area's first postmaster and also sat as a Social Credit member in the Alberta Legislature from 1940 to 1952.

DEL BONITA This hamlet, a port of entry near the Canada–U.S. border, took its name from the Spanish term that means "of the beauty."

D

DELACOUR This hamlet near Calgary was named after a foreman who worked for the Grand Trunk Pacific Railway.

DELBURNE Pop. 641. There are different versions of how this village southeast of Red Deer was named. Perhaps the name came from the first and last syllable of Della Mewburn's name. She was the sister of Dr. F.H. Mewburn, a pioneer medical worker. On the other hand, perhaps the name (at times spelled "Delbourne") was selected from a list of names offered to the settlers.

DELIA Pop. 208. This village took its name from the wife of local businessman A.L. Davis. An informal restaurant/boarding house in the area was known as Delia's Stopping House. Delia is about 30 km west of Hanna.

DELTA GLACIER This glacier about 95 km northwest of Banff took its name from the delta found at the end of nearby Delta Creek.

DELTAFORM MOUNTAIN (3424 m) This is a descriptive name for this mountain, which has a form resembling the Greek letter Δ, delta. Deltaform Mountain is about 50 km west-northwest of Banff, adjacent to the Valley of the Ten Peaks.

DERWENT Pop. 110. This village was named by the Canadian Pacific Railway after Derwentwater, England. The name appears in England as far back as 730, when Bede, a great scholar during the early Middle Ages, mentioned *Deruuentionist fluuii*, meaning "Derwent River." Derwent, Alberta, is near Elk Point.

DEVILS HEAD (2997 m) This mountain took its name from the Cree name *we-ti-kwos-ti-kwan*. Sir George Simpson noted the mountain has "a rude resemblance to an upturned face." Devils Head is near Banff.

DEVON Pop. 4496. This community southwest of Edmonton came into being after the discovery of the Leduc oilfield in 1947. It was a company town and was named after the geological formation in which the oil was found. Devon was incorporated as a town in 1950.

D

DEVON MOUNTAIN (3004 m) This mountain has a Devonian geological formation. Devon Mountain is about 75 km northwest of Banff.

DEWBERRY Pop. 185. This village took its name from the dewberry. Apparently, indecision among settlers in choosing a name for their community ended when a lady walked into the local store with a bucket of dewberries and suggested that the name of the berry, common to the parklands of Alberta, would make a good name for the village. Dewberry is about 45 km northeast of Vermilion.

DIADEM PEAK (3371 m) The name for this mountain refers to the crown, or diadem, of snow on the peak. Diadem Peak is 77 km south-southeast of Jasper.

DIAMOND CITY Pop. 179. The first name chosen for this hamlet near Lethbridge was Black Diamond Mine, referring to coal, the area's economic backbone. However, that name was already taken, so the name was shortened to Diamond City.

DICKSON Pop. 70. This hamlet was named after Dickson Creek, which took the name of an early settler from Norway, Mr. Benedickson. Dickson is about 24 km west of Innisfail.

DIDSBURY Pop. 3553. This town took its name from Didsbury, Manchester, England. Didsbury is of ancient origin, being recorded as *Dedisbiry* and *Diddesbiru* in the 1200s. The name of this community is English, but its first settlers were Mennonite. Didsbury, approximately 70 km southwest of Red Deer, was incorporated as a town in 1906.

D

DINOSAUR PARK This provincial park was established in 1955 and is one of the best sources of Cretaceous dinosaur fossils in the world. Some 70 million years ago this area was a habitat for dinosaurs. The park has been declared a UNESCO World Heritage Site. Dinosaur Park is about 100 km northwest of Medicine Hat. (see Patricia)

DINOSAUR RIDGE This ridge about 77 km northwest of Grande Cache resembles the shape of a dinosaur.

DIP SLOPE MOUNTAIN (3125 m) This descriptive name refers to the dip on the southwest slope of the mountain. Dip Slope Mountain is about 75 km northwest of Banff.

DISASTER POINT There are a couple of versions of how this point received its name. One story has it that some horses travelling on the trail to Jasper House lost their footing here and fell down the steep cliff. Another tale suggests that Surveyor General Dr. E.G. Deville chose this name, perhaps jokingly, because Sandford Fleming's brandy flask broke on a rock here. Sir Sandford Fleming was engaged in the Canadian Pacific Survey, conducted from 1871 to 1876, which sought a route through the Rockies for the transcontinental CPR line.

DIVISION MOUNTAIN (3030 m) The name for this mountain describes its location on the Alberta–British Columbia boundary. Division Mountain is about 130 km northwest of Banff.

DIXONVILLE This hamlet near Grimshaw was named after Roy and Ethel Dixon, operators of the general store and post office in the community. The post office was opened in 1930.

DOGPOUND This locality received its name in 1883, but the source of the name is unknown. Perhaps it was derived from the Cree name *mizekampehpoocaha*, meaning "wolf caught in buffalo pound." But the most likely explanation for the name Dogpound is from the pounding of dogs' paws on the frozen creek when Native hunting parties returned to their winter camps.

DOLOMITE PEAK (2782 m) This mountain peak took its name from the Dolomites, a mountain range in the Italian Alps. Dolomite Peak is about 80 km northwest of Banff.

D

DONALDA Pop. 241. This village near Bashaw was named after Donalda Crossway, the niece of railway executive Sir Donald Mann. The village was incorporated in 1912 and was previously known as Harker and then Eidswold.

DONATVILLE Pop. 14. This hamlet near Athabasca was named after Donat Gingras, an early settler in the area.

DONNELLY Pop. 403. It is believed this village was named after an official of the Edmonton, Dunvegan and British Columbia Railway. The village was officially incorporated in 1956.

DORMER MOUNTAIN (2766 m) This name describes the mountain's ridges, which meet in right angles and form the shape of dormer windows. Dormer Mountain is about 50 km north of Banff.

DOROTHY This hamlet near Drumheller was named after the first, and for many years the only, baby born in the district. Dorothy Wilson was the daughter of rancher Jack Wilson. The post office opened here in 1908.

DOUAI MOUNTAIN (3120 m) This mountain took its name from Douai, a fortified town in France. The name commemorates the capture of this European town in 1918 by Canadian and other Allied troops. Douai Mountain is located about 145 km northwest of Banff.

DRACO PEAK (2587 m) This is a descriptive name for this mountain, which resembles a dragon. *Draco* is Latin for "dragon." Draco Peak is located about 125 km northwest of Jasper.

D

DRAPER This locality near Fort McMurray was named after Thomas Draper, an early oil sands entrepreneur. During the 1920s, some of his research projects included using oil sands as a paving material. One of his paving contracts was for a section of Wellington Street in Ottawa.

DRAYTON VALLEY Pop. 5883. This oil town was named after an English village in Hampshire, England. It was the hometown of the wife of postmaster W.J. Drake. Drayton Valley was incorporated as a town in 1957. Before 1920, it was known as Powerhouse.

DRIFTPILE RIVER The name for this river about 58 km west of Slave Lake is descriptive of the many piles of driftwood that collect in the river.

DRUMHELLER Pop. 7883. This city was named after a pioneer of the Alberta coal fields, Samuel Drumheller (1864–1925). Born in Washington State, he moved to Alberta and, in 1910, bought the land that is now the townsite of Drumheller. He opened a coal mine there in 1918. Today, the city is the home of the Royal Tyrrell Museum of Palaeontology. The world-class museum centres on the theme "A Celebration of Life" and covers 3. 5 billion years of life on Earth. The Dinosaur Hall has more than 35 complete dinosaur skeletons. In addition to impressive murals throughout the museum, there are 800 fossil specimens on display. The museum has about 110,000 fossil specimens in its collection.

DRY ISLAND BUFFALO JUMP PROVINCIAL PARK This park about 35 km northeast of Three Hills was established in 1975. In addition to containing a buffalo jump, it has a large hill that is bordered by a dry river channel on one side and the Red Deer River on the other side. This hill gives the park the "dry island" part of its name.

DUCHESS Pop. 693. The village of Duchess, approximately 117 km northwest of Medicine Hat, was named in honour of the Duchess of Connaught, wife of the Duke of Connaught and Strathearn. The Duke of Connaught, a large landowner in the area, served as governor general from 1911 to 1916. (see Empress)

D

DUFFIELD The Canadian Northern Railway opened a station here in 1911 and named it after George Duffield Hall of Boston, Massachusetts. The hamlet of Duffield is located about 23 km west of Stony Plain.

DUHAMEL Pop. less than 100. This hamlet was named after the Most Reverend Joseph Thomas Duhamel, the Roman Catholic archbishop of Ottawa, who gave the local priest a church bell. In the late 1800s, this settlement centred around a trading post known to the Cree as *notikiwn sipi*, meaning "Battle River." The place was also called Battle River Crossing, because it was a place where the river could be forded. Duhamel is southwest of Camrose.

DUNMORE This hamlet close to Medicine Hat took its name from the Seventh Earl of Dunmore, Charles A. Murray. The earl had major holdings in the Canadian Agricultural Coal and Colonization Company. Dunmore was previously called Coleridge.

DUNVEGAN This hamlet was the site of a North West Company (NWC) post, Fort Dunvegan, established in 1805 by Archibald Norman McLeod (possibly the namesake of McLeod River). McLeod named the post after his ancestral home of Dunvegan, a castle on the Isle of Skye. The castle has been the home of Clan McLeod since 1200. Dunvegan, Alberta, is located about 85 km north of Grande Prairie.

DUVERNAY This hamlet near Two Hills was named in honour of Ludger Duvernay, who founded the Société St. Jean Baptiste in 1834. Duvernay was previously known as South Bend.

E

EAGLESHAM This village about 90 km northeast of Grande Prairie was likely named after Eaglesham, Renfrewshire, Scotland.

EAST COULEE Pop. 157. The name of this hamlet near Drumheller describes the location of the community. A coulee is a ravine, usually dry, that has been eroded or worn away by rain and melting snow.

EBON PEAK (2910 m) This name refers to the ebony-coloured line that runs through the snow-covered peaks in the area. Ebon Peak is about 100 km northwest of Banff.

ECKVILLE Pop. 901. This town was named after A.E.T. Eckford, an early settler in the area. Eckville is about 40 km west-northwest of Red Deer.

EDBERG Pop. 137. This village near Camrose was named for Johan A. Edstrom, its first postmaster and a local businessman. He took the first part of his name, "Ed," and combined it with *berg* (the Swedish word meaning "hill") to form "Edberg." The village was incorporated in 1930.

EDEN PEAK (3180 m) The origin for the name of this peak is not certain. Eden Peak is about 80 km south-southeast of Jasper.

EDGERTON Pop. 372. This village near Wainwright was named after H.H. Edgerton, a Grand Trunk Pacific Railway engineer.

EDMONTON Metropolitan pop. 1,016,000. Edmonton started more than 200 years ago when the Hudson's Bay

Company and the North West Company built fur-trading posts in the area in 1795. When the two companies merged in 1821, Fort Edmonton became the leading centre for the western fur trade. Edmonton House was likely named after Edmonton (near London, England), the birthplace of a clerk at the fort. According to the *Oxford Dictionary of English Place Names*, Edmonton appears in the *Domesday Book* of 1086 as *Adelmentone*. The Cree named Edmonton *amiskwachie*, meaning "beaver hills house," after the nearby Beaver Hills. Following floods, Fort Edmonton was moved in 1830 to higher ground, near the location of today's Alberta Legislative Building. The fort served as an economic centre for pioneers heading north and west. In 1892, Edmonton became a town. During the Klondike Gold Rush of 1897, the town boomed as prospectors headed north in search of gold. In 1904, Edmonton was incorporated as a city. Edmonton's geographic location, where the North Saskatchewan River comes close to the Athabasca River, its resource-rich environs and its early start made the city the economic and political centre of central and north Alberta. In 1905, Edmonton was named the provincial capital.

E

With the gold rush far behind, Edmonton continued to grow as a strategic transportation and service centre, and in the 1940s it became known as the "Gateway to the North." The discovery of the Leduc oilfield just after World War II and the subsequent oil boom developed Edmonton as the base for most of the province's oil production. Edmonton boasts the largest recreational river valley park in North America. It covers 7400 hectares and boasts 112 kilometres of biking, walking and equine trails. The city's non-stop celebrations throughout the summer have earned Edmonton the reputation of Canada's "Festival City." Edmonton is located 300 km north of Calgary and is close to the centre of the province.

E

EDSON Pop. 7399. This town west of Edmonton was named after Edson J. Chamberlain, vice-president and general manager of the Grand Trunk Pacific Railway. Chamberlain later became president of Grand Trunk Railway. Edson was previously known as Heatherwood.

EDWAND This locality near Smoky Lake was named after its first postmaster, Edward Anderson. The name is a combination of the first three letters in "Edward" and the first three letters in "Anderson."

EGREMONT This hamlet near Redwater took its name from a town in Cumberland, England. The wife of R.C. Armstrong, its first postmaster, hailed from this English town.

EGYPT LAKE Egypt Lake is located about 25 km southwest of Banff. The origin of the name is uncertain, although it may be because of the lake's proximity to Pharaoh Peaks.

EIFFEL PEAK (3084 m) A natural rock tower resembling the Eiffel Tower in Paris rises from this mountain. Eiffel Peak is about 50 km west-northwest of Banff.

EISENHOWER PEAK (2862 m) In 1979, this peak on the east end of Castle Mountain was named in honour of General Dwight D. Eisenhower, who commanded the Allied Forces in Europe during World War II. This peak was named at the same time the name of Mount Eisenhower was changed back to Castle Mountain. Eisenhower Peak is about 28 km northwest of Banff.

ELBOW RIVER This river flowing eastward from the Rockies to Calgary took its name from the sharp, abrupt turn it makes as it flows into the Bow River at Calgary.

ELEPHAS MOUNTAIN (2940 m) *Elephas* is Latin for "elephant." This mountain took its name from its shape, which resembles an elephant's head. Elephas Mountain is about 36 km southwest of Jasper.

ELK ISLAND NATIONAL PARK This park about 45 km east of Edmonton was set aside as a wildlife reserve by the Canadian government in 1913. Its lakes and forests provide a sanctuary for many species of animals and plants. Among the inhabitants in the park are imported plains and wood bison. There are about 650 plains bison and about 400 wood bison in the park. In the 1700s, an estimated 60 million plains bison roamed the North American plains. One hundred years later they had been brought to the brink of extinction by overhunting.

ELK POINT Pop. 1492. This town is located about 90 km north-northwest of Lloydminster. It was likely named after Elk Point, South Dakota.

ELKWATER Pop. 52. This hamlet about 45 km southeast of Medicine Hat, inside Cypress Hills Provincial Park, took its name from the Blackfoot word *ponokiokwe*. A great number of elk and deer gather to drink water from nearby Elkwater Lake. The elk and deer were hunted to extinction in the late 1800s. Elk were re-introduced to the area in 1938.

ELLERSLIE The name of this railway point within the south city limits of Edmonton has two possible sources. It may have been named after a Scottish manor belonging to Sir William Wallace, or it may have been named after a character in a novel by Sir Walter Scott.

ELLIOTT PEAK (2872 m) This mountain peak was named after Elliot Barnes. The son of a local rancher, he climbed this mountain when he was just eight years old. Elliott Peak is 125 km northwest of Banff.

ELLSCOT Pop. 11. A post office opened here in 1916 and was named after L. Scott, of the Alberta & Great Waterways Railway. Ellscot, a hamlet, is approximately 34 km southeast of Athabasca.

E

ELNORA Pop. 278. The name of this village is taken from the first names of Elinor Hogg and Nora Edwards, the wives of its first postmasters. Elnora is about 32 km north of Three Hills and was incorporated in 1929.

ELPOCA MOUNTAIN (3029 m) Elpoca Mountain, at the head of the Elbow River and Pocaterra Creek, took its name from a combination of the first letters of the names of these water bodies. Elpoca Mountain is about 55 km west of Turner Valley.

ELYSIUM MOUNTAIN (2446 m) The name for this mountain overlooking fine meadows refers to a mythological place. In Greek mythology, Elysium is the destination of blessed people after their death. Elysium Mountain is near Jasper.

EMIGRANTS MOUNTAIN (2553 m) This mountain was named after the many people from California and eastern Canada who took part in BC's Cariboo Gold Rush. Emigrants Mountain is near Jasper.

EMPRESS Pop. 186. This village 108 km northwest of Medicine Hat was named for Queen Victoria, Empress of India. Her Majesty was given this title after the Indian Mutiny (1856–57) was put down. Empress is on the rail line that became known as the "Royal Line," running from Empress to Bassano (named after an Italian count). Names along the route also include Countess, Duchess and Patricia.

ENCHANT The name of this hamlet likely reflected the feelings of the area's pioneers who were "enchanted" with their new community. Enchant is about 56 km northeast of Lethbridge. It was previously known as Lost Lake.

END MOUNTAIN (2420 m) This mountain was named for the fact it is situated at the end of a mountain range. End Mountain is near Canmore.

ENDIANG Pop. 21. The post office opened in this hamlet in 1910 and took its name from the Chippewa word for "my home." Endiang is approximately 38 km northeast of Hanna.

ENILDA This hamlet near High Prairie took its name from the wife of its first postmaster, J. Tompkins. Her first name, Adline, was reversed in spelling to form the name.

ENSIGN This hamlet commemorates the Red Ensign, at the time the official flag of Canada. In 1965, the flag was replaced by the Maple Leaf flag. Ensign is about 60 km southeast of Calgary.

ENTRANCE This locality, once a busy railway stop, is at the entrance to Jasper National Park.

ENTWISTLE Pop. 453. This village about 96 km west of Edmonton was named after James G. Entwistle, an early settler and first postmaster. Entwistle was incorporated as a village in 1955.

EON MOUNTAIN (3310 m) It is thought this name refers to the eons that have passed during the elevation of the mountain. Eon Mountain is about 105 km southwest of Calgary.

EPAULETTE MOUNTAIN (3059 m) This mountain 110 km northwest of Banff resembles an epaulette on a uniform. It was previously known as Pyramid Mountain.

EREBUS MOUNTAIN (3119 m) The name for this mountain describes its dark rock. *Erebus* is the Greek word for "darkness." Erebus Mountain is about 30 km southwest of Jasper.

EREMITE MOUNTAIN (2910 m) This mountain's isolation gave it its name. An eremite is a hermit. This mountain is located about 30 km southwest of Jasper.

E

ERSKINE Pop. 335. It is believed this hamlet near Stettler was named after Lady Millicent Fanny St. Claire-Erskine. She was married to the Fourth Duke of Sutherland, who had landholdings in Alberta. (see Millicent)

ESPLANADE MOUNTAIN (2292 m) The descriptive name of this mountain about 23 km north-northwest of Jasper refers to its flat-topped feature.

ETZIKOM The name of this hamlet came from the Blackfoot term meaning "valley," though the Blackfoot called this location *misloonsisco*, meaning "Crow Springs." Crow Natives obtained water from the area's springs. Etzikom is about 67 km southwest of Medicine Hat.

EVANSBURG This village about 39 km south of Mayerthorpe was named for Henry Marshall E. Evans (1876–1973). In 1900, he moved from Toronto to Winnipeg where he became business manager of the *Winnipeg Tribune*. In 1904, he settled in Edmonton, becoming president of the Edmonton Board of Trade and later the city's mayor. During his term in office, he successfully negotiated a bond issue, saving the city from a financial crisis. Evans also served as a financial advisor to the Alberta government in 1931. In 1946, he became an officer of the Order of the British Empire, in recognition of his meritorious service during World War II.

EXCEL This locality approximately 154 km east of Drumheller took its name from the excellent geographical location of the community and from the enthusiasm felt by the settlers for the potential of the townsite. A post office opened in Excel in 1911.

EXCOFFIN BOTTOM This area was named in honour of John Excoffin, a French immigrant who moved to the Lethbridge area in 1902 and settled in the Oldman River valley floor (bottom). Excoffin gained a reputation for being eccentric. For example, he played a French horn to call his cattle into the farmyard at the end of their day in pasture. It is said the cattle came running on getting their cues from Excoffin's horn. If the wind was right, neighbours within several kilometres could also enjoy Excoffin's French horn. It is not known if neighbours hearing the notes from Excoffin's horn moved as quickly as his cows towards his homestead.

E

EXCELSIOR MOUNTAIN (2744 m) This mountain took its name from its great height. Excelsior Mountain is near Jasper.

EXSHAW Pop. 374. Sir Sandford Fleming, a prominent land surveyor and director of the Western Canada Cement and Coal Company, named this hamlet after his son-in-law, Lord Exshaw. Exshaw is near Canmore.

EXSHAW MOUNTAIN (1783 m) This mountain near Canmore took its name from the hamlet of the same name. (see Exshaw)

F

FABYAN This hamlet near Wainwright was named after the summer resort of Fabyan, New Hampshire. It is thought the community in New Hampshire was named after Robert Fabyan (?–1513), author of *The Concordance of Histories*, also known as *The New Chronicles of England and France*, which was published in 1516 and covers the history of England from the time of Brutus to 1400 AD.

FAIRVIEW Pop. 3316. This is a descriptive name for the town located about 71 km west-southwest of Peace River. The name was established in the district by H.L. Propst, an early settler who named his homestead Fairview. The name was later used in Fairview Municipal District #858. The decision of railway planners to bypass Waterhole, six kilometres south, and set up a siding at this location was an important factor in the development of this townsite. Most of the buildings were moved from Waterhole to Fairview to be closer to the railway siding.

FAIRVIEW MOUNTAIN (2744 m) This mountain about 55 km northwest of Banff took its name from the splendid view available at its summit.

FALHER Pop. 1149. This town was named in honour of Father Constant Falher, a Roman Catholic Oblate missionary. In 1912, Mission St. Jean Baptiste de Falher opened some five km away. Three years later, the Edmonton, Dunvegan and British Columbia Railway built a station nearby and took the mission's name, when it started this town.

FALLIS This hamlet was named after W.S. Fallis, an executive of the Sherwin-Williams Company of Canada. Fallis is about 43 km west-northwest of Stony Plain.

FALUN This hamlet was named after a copper-mining town in Sweden. Many of the early settlers in this community near Wetaskiwin came from Falun.

FARBUS MOUNTAIN (3150 m) This mountain about 140 km northwest of Banff was named after the French village of Farbus. Canadian troops fought in the vicinity of this village during the World War I Battle of Vimy.

FATIGUE MOUNTAIN (2959 m) This name was chosen by W.S. Drewery to describe his feelings after climbing this mountain. Fatique Mountain is near Banff.

FAUST Pop. 343. This hamlet about 56 km west of Slave Lake was named after E.T. Faust, a locomotive engineer on the Edmonton, Dunvegan and British Columbia Railway.

FAWCETT Pop. 118. This hamlet took its name from an engineer during construction of the Edmonton, Dunvegan and British Columbia Railway. Fawcett is about 45 km northwest of Westlock.

FERINTOSH Pop. 130. This village was named after the barony of Ferintosh in Scotland. The name was proposed by area resident Dr. J.R. McLeod, a member of the first Alberta Legislature (1905–09). Ferintosh is located near Camrose.

FESTUBERT MOUNTAIN (2522 m) This mountain was named after the French village of Festubert, where Canadian troops fought in 1915. Festubert Mountain is near Waterton Lakes National Park.

FIDDLE PEAK (2243 m) This mountain about 30 km south-southwest of Hinton was officially named in 1960 after nearby Fiddle Range. (see Fiddle Range)

FIDDLE RANGE There are different versions of how this mountain range was named. Apparently wind blowing through the range sounds like fiddle music. Also the shape

F

of the nearby Athabasca River has been likened to the shape of a fiddle. Fiddle Range and Fiddle Peak are located about 30 km south-southwest of Hinton.

FIFTH MERIDIAN There are six meridians (north-south baselines) in the Dominion Land Survey laid out in the late 1800s. The First, or Prime Meridian, is near Winnipeg; the Fourth Meridian forms the border between Alberta and Saskatchewan. The hamlet of Fifth Meridian took its name from the fact it is located on the Fifth Meridian. The community is about 180 km northeast of High Level.

FITZGERALD This hamlet about 340 km north of Fort McMurray was named in 1915 in honour of RNWMP Inspector Francis Joseph Fitzgerald. Inspector Fitzgerald, along with Constables Kenny and Taylor and former Constable Carter, lost their lives while patrolling between Fort McPherson and Dawson City. Evidence surfaced that the patrol did not have enough food for the journey and that their guide became lost. Fitzgerald was formerly known as Smith Landing.

FLATBUSH Pop. 38. This hamlet took its name from the flat countryside and the abundance of trees in the area. Flatbush is about 55 km west of Athabasca.

FLEET There are various possible sources for the name of this hamlet near Castor, in central Alberta. Perhaps the name honours the British Fleet, or perhaps the hamlet was named for the fleet of ships owned by the Canadian Pacific Railway.

FOLDING MOUNTAIN (2844 m) This mountain about 25 km south-southwest of Hinton took its name from its "folded" rock strata.

FOREMOST Pop. 556. In 1913, a new rail line from Lethbridge to Weyburn, Saskatchewan, stopped in Foremost, so at the time Foremost was the "foremost" point of the rails. Another story claims the hamlet is first and "foremost" the friendliest place in the area. Foremost is about 80 km southwest of Medicine Hat.

FORESTBURG Pop. 930. There are different accounts of how this village 171 km southeast of Edmonton was named. Possibly it was named for Forestburg, South Dakota, the hometown of an early settler, or maybe it was named for Forestburg, Ontario, the hometown of other area residents.

F

FORGETMENOT MOUNTAIN (2332 m) This mountain took its name from the forget-me-not flower found in the area. Forgetmenot Mountain is located about 50 km southwest of Calgary.

FORGETMENOT PASS The name was derived from the forget-me-not flowers growing in the area. This pass is located 52 km southwest of Grande Cache (and is nowhere near Forgetmenot Mountain).

FORT ASSINIBOINE This hamlet is located 58 km southeast of Swan Hills, on the Athabasca River. This post, established in 1823 by the Hudson's Bay Company, was likely named after the Assiniboine people. The post was at the end of a long portage from Fort Edmonton. From this point, travellers could go down the Athabasca River, ending up eventually in the Arctic Ocean, or upstream, eventually arriving at Fort Vancouver via the Athabasca Pass.

FORT CHIPEWYAN Pop. 935. This hamlet, believed to be the first white settlement in what is now Alberta (tied with Fort Vermilion), took its name from the people who lived in the area, the Chipewyan.

MORE ABOUT FORT CHIPEWYAN... *Fort Chipewyan was set up as a trading post on Lake Athabasca in 1788. Some say the post was second only to Fort William (on Lake Superior) in importance as a fur-trading centre. Fort Chipewyan prospered and took on*

F

a couple of nicknames, "the Emporium of the North" and "Little Athens" because of the amenities it offered despite its wilderness surroundings. The original site established by Roderick Mackenzie of the North West Company was abandoned in 1804 with the setting up of a new site on the north shore of the lake. Apparently, the move put the North West Company in a better position to trade with the Chipewyan. Chipewyan is a Cree word that was translated as "pointed skins," referring to the pointed tunics the people wore.

FORT KENT Pop. 163. This hamlet was named after Fort Kent in the U.S. state of Maine. Fort Kent is near Bonnyville.

FORT MacKAY Pop. 347. This hamlet about 57 km north-northwest of Fort McMurray was named in honour of Dr. William Morrison MacKay (1836–1917). Dr. MacKay, originally from Scotland, was a surgeon with the Hudson's Bay Company. He was also a fur trader, a chief trader and factor at various locations, such as Fort Rae, Fort Resolution, Fort Simpson, Dunvegan and Fort Chipewyan. After his retirement from the Hudson's Bay Company, Dr. MacKay took up private medical practice in Edmonton and assisted in founding the Northern Alberta Medical Association.

FORT MACLEOD Pop. 3034. Fort Macleod was named after Lieutenant-Colonel James Farquharson Macleod (1836–94). The town of Fort Macleod is located 40 km west of Lethbridge.

MORE ABOUT LIEUTENANT-COLONEL MACLEOD... *James Macleod established the first North-West Mounted Police post in Alberta following the "Great March of 1874." The main objective of the NWMP was to put an end to the illegal whiskey trade, something that was successfully accomplished by Macleod and his men. He* *also negotiated Treaty 7 with the Blackfoot, Sarcee and Stoney Natives. He later became commissioner of the NWMP. Upon retirement, Lieutenant-Colonel Macleod was appointed a magistrate and in 1887 he was named a judge of the Supreme Court of the North-West Territories. Area Natives knew him as "Bull's head" because of a buffalo head that was over the entrance to his residence. The crest of the clan Macleod contains a bull's head.*

F

FORT McMURRAY Pop. 36,9663. This community took its name from William McMurray. He was chief factor for the Hudson's Bay Company when the company established a trading post in 1870 at this spot, where the Clearwater River runs into the Athabasca River. In the 1920s, efforts were made to extract and separate oil from the tar sands in the area (see Bitumount). In 1996, Fort McMurray dropped its official status as a city and became an urban service area within the specialized Municipality of Wood Buffalo (with a population of 79,810). Fort McMurray is 378 km northeast of Edmonton.

MORE ABOUT FORT McMURRAY...*Fort McMurray's economy is based on the Athabasca Oil Sands. It is estimated that the Fort McMurray region contains 1.7 to 2.5 trillion barrels of oil, of which 300 billion barrels are recoverable from the tar sands with current technology. This amount compares to the 261 billion barrels available in Saudi Arabia.*

In 1964, the building of the Great Canadian Oil Sands project signaled the commercialization of tapping the huge oil reserves. Since the building of this first commercial plant, other oil sands megaprojects, such as the one belonging to Syncrude, have been extracting synthetic crude oil from the tar sands. The synthetic crude from Fort McMurray supplies a significant part of Canada's oil needs.

F

FORT SASKATCHEWAN Pop. 13,109. This city is on the site of the first North-West Mounted Police post in the district, set up in 1875 by Inspector W.D. Jarvis. Edmontonians complained the post was not located in their community, but at the time, the CPR's transcontinental line was expected to be built along the North Saskatchewan River and then through the Yellowhead Pass. Fort Saskatchewan was built where the railway was expected to cross the river. Jarvis thought it efficient to build the post close to the proposed railway line. The police post was named after the nearby (North) Saskatchewan River (see North Saskatchewan River). However, the CPR transcontinental crossed the southern prairies instead, and no rail line was built through the area until 30 years later. The Fort Saskatchewan Museum located in the downtown of the city has various historic buildings, including Fort Saskatchewan's first courthouse. Fort Saskatchewan is about 35 km northeast of Edmonton.

FORT VERMILION Pop. 775. This settlement about 67 km east-southeast of High Level is the oldest European settlement in Alberta (tied with Fort Chipewyan). It was established in 1788 as the main post of the North West Company on the Peace River between Fort Chipewyan and Fort Dunvegan. In 1821, the Hudson's Bay Company took over Fort Vermilion, and some years later, moved it to the present site of the town of Fort Vermilion. The name Vermilion is believed to refer to the red ochre (iron-impregnated clay) found in the area. Distant Vermilion and Redwater are also named after iron deposits.

FORTALICE MOUNTAIN (2835 m) This is a descriptive name for this mountain, which looks like a small fort. "Fortalice" is an archaic word for "small fort." Fortalice Mountain is near Jasper.

FORTRESS, THE (3000 m) This mountain 83 km west-southwest of Calgary took its name from its resemblance to a fortress. It was previously known as The Tower, but the name was changed to avoid duplication with Tower Mountain.

FORUM PEAK (2415 m) This peak near Waterton Lakes National Park was named for its curving walls that resemble a forum.

FOSSIL MOUNTAIN (2946 m) This mountain took its name from the large number of fossils found in the limestone of the mountain. Fossil Mountain is 50 km northwest of Banff.

FOX CREEK Pop. 2321. This town about 75 km northwest of Whitecourt was named after the nearby creek of the same name. The creek was named after the type of animal commonly found in the area.

FOX LAKE This hamlet about 150 km east of High Level took its name from its location in the Fox Lake Indian Reserve. The origin for the name of nearby Fox Lake is unknown.

FRANCHÈRE PEAK (2812 m) This mountain was named after Gabriel Franchère. He wrote the first published account of a journey through the Rockies in *Relation d'un voyage à la Coté du Nord-Ouest de l'Amérique Septentrionale dans les années 1810, 11, 12, et 14.* Franchère Peak is near Jasper. (see Mount Lapensée)

FRANK Pop. 6500 (estimated). This former village near Blairmore, 220 km west of Calgary, was named in 1901 after A.L. Frank, the owner of the region's first coal mine. Frank was consolidated with other Crowsnest Pass communities to form the Municipality of Crowsnest Pass in 1979. In 1903, Frank was the site of a tremendous rock slide that crashed down from Turtle Mountain.

F

F

MORE ABOUT FRANK... The Frank Slide, at 4:10 AM on April 29, 1903, buried one end of the village of Frank and claimed 70 lives. An estimated 90 million tonnes of limestone came tumbling down and covered about three km of the valley to a depth of more than 30 metres. In one of the world's most destructive rock slides, it only took about 100 seconds for the giant wedge of limestone to slip from the north face of Turtle Mountain and cross the valley. Coal miners working the nightshift inside the mountain were trapped by the slide. It took them 14 hours of hard work to dig themselves out. No workers in the mine were killed. A week after the disaster, the mine reopened. It closed for good in 1911. Some believe the mineshafts weakened the mountain and helped cause the slide, but many scientists are puzzled as to what caused the disaster at Turtle Mountain. The Natives in the area had long been cautious about "The Mountain that Walks." They never camped at its foot.

FRESNOY MOUNTAIN (3240 m) This mountain 120 km southeast of Jasper was named after Fresnoy, France, which Canadian troops captured in 1917.

FROG LAKE The name of this lake was derived from its Cree place name. At the start of the Riel Rebellion in 1885, a Cree band lead by Big Bear massacred nine white settlers at this lake. Frog Lake is about 30 km east of Drayton Valley.

G

GABLE MOUNTAIN (2928 m) This mountain was named for its long ridge that resembles the gable on a house. Gable Mountain is 55 km north-northwest of Banff.

GADSBY Pop. 40. Incorporated in 1910, this village was named after M.F. Gadsby of Ottawa. Gadsby is 25 km east of Stettler.

GAINFORD Pop. 104. This hamlet near Drayton Valley was named after a town in Durham, England. It was previously known as Seba.

GALAHAD Pop. 175. This village is likely named after the famous knight of the Round Table. Galahad is near Forestburg.

GARGOYLE MOUNTAIN (2693 m) This is a descriptive name for this mountain, which has gargoyle-shaped features. A gargoyle is a grotesquely carved architectural decorative figure that sometimes is set up as a waterspout. Gargoyle Mountain is near Jasper.

GHOST RIVER This river about 50 km northwest of Calgary took its name from death and ghosts in the area. According to Peter Erasmus, who was a noted guide on the Palliser Expedition, a ghost was seen going up and down the river picking up skulls after a battle between the Cree and an unnamed enemy.

GIANT STEPS The descriptive name for this cascade (a series of waterfalls) refers to its step-like features. Giant Steps is located about 55 km west-northwest of Banff.

GIBBON PASS (2256 m) This mountain near Banff was named after John Murray Gibbon (1875–1952), a journalist and author.

GIBBONS Pop. 2748. This town near Edmonton was named after local pioneer William Reynolds Gibbons. He came west from Ontario in 1892. Gibbons was known as Astleyville and Battenburg before the community adopted this name in 1920.

G

GIBRALTAR MOUNTAIN (2655 m) This mountain about 40 km southwest of Turner Valley bears a resemblance to the Rock of Gibraltar.

GIBRALTER ROCK (2879 m) This mountain about 55 km northwest of Turner Valley was so named because of its resemblance to the Rock of Gibraltar. (The spelling error comes from the original naming.)

GIROUXVILLE Pop. 332. This village was named in honour of the Giroux family, pioneers of the district. It was previously known as Fowler. Girouxville is near Falher.

GLACIER LAKE This is a descriptive name for this lake, which is fed by a glacial stream. Glacier Lake is about 120 km northwest of Banff.

GLEICHEN This hamlet was named after a German count, Albert Edward W. Gleichen. He was a financial backer of the Canadian Pacific Railway. Gleichen is about 65 km southeast of Calgary.

MORE ABOUT GLEICHEN..._Located near Gleichen is the Siksika Nation Museum of Natural History. The permanent galleries show a wide range of Blackfoot (Siksika) artifacts from Stone Age relics to contemporary arts and crafts._

GLENDON Pop. 418. This village near Bonnyville was named for the maiden name of the mother of its first postmaster, J.P. Spencer.

GLENEVIS This hamlet was named after Glennevis, Cape Breton Island, Nova Scotia. Glenevis (the second "n" was omitted) is about 37 km south-southwest of Barrhead.

GLENWOOD Pop. 295. This village 60 km southwest of Lethbridge was named Glenwoodville in 1908 after Glen Wood, the first-born son of Edward Wood. Edward Wood was president of the Alberta Stake, formerly the Cochrane Ranch, which had been purchased by the Mormons in 1906. At the request of the postal service, the name was changed to Glenwood in 1979.

G

GOLDEN DAYS Pop. 92. It is believed the name of this summer village refers to the "golden days of summer." Golden Days is about 43 km west-northwest of Wetaskiwin.

GOLDEN EAGLE PEAK (3084 m) This mountain about 120 km northwest of Banff took its name from the many golden eagles seen in the area.

GOPHER HEAD This hill about 50 km south-southeast of Stettler resembles the shape of a gopher's head.

GRANDE CACHE Pop. 4441. Fur traders used to hide their goods from thieves by caching their furs for later retrieval. In a specific case, Ignace Giasson of the Hudson's Bay Company was overburdened with furs on a return trip to his fort, and he put them in one large (*grande*) cache at this location. The town of Grande Cache is about 115 km northwest of Hinton.

GRANDE PRAIRIE Pop. 44,631. This city took its name from the name of the prairie in which it is located. The name of this area, the biggest prairie in the region, is made up of the French words for "large plain." Some say Bishop Grouard, a local Roman Catholic Oblate missionary (see Grouard), gave Grande Prairie its name. Others note the Cree referred to the area as *mistahay-muskotoyew*, meaning "big prairie." In the early 1900s, the area, with its fertile soil, developed into an area of farms centred around the growing settlement of Grande Prairie, which became a transportation and service centre for the surrounding district. In the 1970s, the city's economy diversified with the petroleum and forestry industry complementing agriculture. Grande Prairie is about 460 km northwest of Edmonton.

GRANDVIEW Pop. 60. This summer village west of Wetaskiwin took its name from the nearby district of Grandview. It is a descriptive name that refers to the grand view overlooking Watelet Lake that can be seen from the village.

GRANT PASS This pass northwest of Jasper was named after George M. Grant. He was a Presbyterian minister and the secretary for Sir Sandford Fleming's exploration party. Fleming led the Canadian Pacific Survey, conducted from 1871 to 1876, which sought a route through the Rockies for the transcontinental CPR line.

GRANUM Pop. 337. This town took its name from *granum*, the Latin word for "grain." Granum is surrounded by some of the best wheat-growing land in the province. The community won the World's Wheat Crown and several other awards for wheat. Malcolm McKenzie, a Member of Parliament, suggested the town's name, Leavings, be changed to recognize these achievements. The name was officially changed in 1907. (The old name, Leavings, referred to the fact that the community was located where the old Fort Macleod-Calgary Trail left Willow Creek).

GRASSY LAKE This village 80 km east of Lethbridge took its name from the Blackfoot word *moyi-kimi*, meaning "grassy waters." In the translation to English, the place name became Grassy Lake. The village is located along a tributary of the South Saskatchewan River, near a lake that is now dry. The Blackfoot name seems to originate from the presence of water in this region of south Alberta, which the Blackfoot called "much grasses." (A lake by the name of Grassy Lake is located more than 100 km southwest of this village, where it is bisected by the Canada–U.S. border. The lake was known as Wild Horse Lake before 1974, when its name was changed to its Montana name, Grassy Lake.)

GREEN COURT This hamlet was named by its first postmaster, Hamilton Baly. Before arriving in Canada, Baly taught at the King's School in Canterbury, Kent, England, and named his new home after the court outside his old school. Green Court is near Mayerthorpe.

GREEN MOUNTAIN (1844 m) The origin of the name of this mountain near Turner Valley is not certain.

GREENSHIELDS In 1909, this locality near Wainwright was named after E.B. Greenshields, a Montréal businessman and a director of the Grand Trunk Pacific Railway.

GRIMSHAW Pop. 2661. This town near Peace River was named after Dr. M.E. Grimshaw, a medical officer for the Central Canada Railway. In 1914, Dr. Grimshaw set up a medical practice in Peace River country and was later recognized for his tireless service throughout the Peace River district. He served as mayor of Peace River in 1922. Grimshaw owes its origin to the Edmonton, Dunvegan and British Columbia Railway.

GRISETTE MOUNTAIN (2990 m) This mountain took its name from *gris*, which is French for "grey." The name refers to the grey limestone that makes up the mountain. Grisette Mountain is near Jasper.

GROTTO MOUNTAIN (2706 m) This mountain contains a grotto, a small-mouthed high-roofed cave. Grotto Mountain is near Canmore.

GROUARD This hamlet and the nearby Grouard Mission were named after Father Émile Jean-Bapiste Marie Grouard (1840–1931). Starting in 1862, Father Grouard of the Oblate Order served in northern Alberta 66 years. Grouard was vicar apostolic of Athabasca and was consecrated a bishop in 1891. The hamlet of Grouard maintains the Native Cultural Arts Museum that contains collections of artifacts from Natives in many areas of North America. Grouard is about 25 km northeast of High Prairie.

GROVEDALE This hamlet near Grande Prairie took its name from a grove of trees in the vicinity.

GULL LAKE Pop. 149. This summer village near Lacombe is located on the shores of Gull Lake, which was named for the many gulls on the lake.

GUNN This hamlet near Stony Plain was named after Peter Gunn (1864–1927). A Scottish immigrant, Gunn was employed with the Hudson's Bay Company for 27 years, serving as factor at Lac Ste. Anne. He was a Liberal member of the Alberta Legislature from 1909 to 1917.

GUY This hamlet was named in honour of Bishop Joseph Guy, a Roman Catholic Oblate missionary. He became bishop in 1930 and served as the vicar apostolic of Grouard from 1930 to 1937. Guy is about 42 km northwest of High Prairie.

GWYNNE Pop. 127. This hamlet was named after Julia Maude Gwynne, the second wife of Sir Collingwood Schreiber. He followed Sir Sandford Fleming as chief engineer of the Canadian Pacific Railway and later became deputy minister in the federal Railways and Canals department. Schreiber played an important role in the building of the Grand Trunk Pacific Railway.

G

H

HA LING PEAK (2680 m) This peak near Canmore took its name from Ha Ling, a Chinese mineworker. In 1886, Ha Ling won a $50 bet by climbing the mountain within six hours. In 1999, the name of the mountain was changed from Chinaman's Peak to Ha Ling.

HABAY This hamlet about 53 km northeast of Rainbow Lake was named after Father Joseph Charles Leon Marie Habay, OMI. Father Habay served in various missions in northern Alberta, including Grouard.

HADDO PEAK (3070 m) This mountain peak about 55 km west-northwest of Banff was named after Lord Haddo, the eldest son of the Marquess of Aberdeen and Temair.

HAIDUK PEAK (2920 m) There are different versions of how this mountain was named. One theory suggests it was named after the Haiduk district in Hungary. The second possibility is that the peak was named after a village of the same name in Romania. Haiduk Peak is about 28 km southwest of Banff.

HAIG GLACIER This glacier was named after Sir Douglas Haig. He was commander-in-chief of the British Expeditionary Force in France during World War I. Haig Glacier is about 75 km northwest of Turner Valley.

HAIRY HILL This village near Two Hills was named for the hair buffalo once left on shrubs on a nearby hill. In spring, buffalo rub themselves on shrubs and the ground to get rid of their winter fur coat.

HALKIRK Pop. 131. This village was named after Halkirk, Caithnes, Scotland. Halkirk is about 20 km east of Stettler.

HANNA Pop. 3001. This town southeast of Red Deer was named in honour of David Blythe Hanna, who was president of the Canadian National Railway from 1918 to 1922. The CNR, at the time owned by the federal government, took over the many privately owned Canadian railways that went bankrupt during World War I. Hanna had a long career in the railway business, being also associated with the Grand Trunk, the New York West Shore and Buffalo Railway, the Manitoba and Northwestern Railway and the Lake Manitoba Railway and Canal Company.

H

HARDISTY Pop. 808. This town was named after Richard Hardisty. Like his father and grandfather, Richard Hardisty (1831–89) worked as chief factor for the Hudson's Bay Company. He was chief factor at Edmonton House (Fort Edmonton) from 1872 to 1882. He was appointed to the Senate in 1888, the first senator to hail from what would be the province of Alberta, but he died the following year. The town of Hardisty is 110 km southeast of Camrose. Mount Hardisty is also named after him.

HARMATTAN This hamlet was given its name by the Canadian Postal Service. It was named after a hot parching wind that blows in northeast Africa during the winter months. Harmattan is near Sundre.

HARVEY PASS This pass 17 km southwest of Banff was named after Ralph L. Harvey. He was the first person to cross the pass in winter.

HAT MOUNTAIN (1800 m) One peak of this mountain 55 km northwest of Grande Cache resembles a hat.

HAY LAKES Pop. 352. This village southeast of Edmonton took its name from a nearby lake. The lake was known by the Cree as a *pi chi koo ohi was*, meaning "little swamp."

HAYS Pop. less than 100. There are various sources for the name of this hamlet about 80 km west of Medicine Hat. It may have been named after a manager of the Canada Land and Irrigation Co., David Hays, or perhaps it was named after the president of the Grand Trunk and the Grand Trunk Pacific Railway, Melville Hays.

HAYTER This hamlet near Provost was named after Hayter Reed, manager of the Canadian Pacific Railway hotels. He also held senior positions in the federal Department of Indian Affairs.

H

HAZELDINE This hamlet was named after Hazeldean, Sussex, England. Hazeldine is about 37 km northeast of Vermilion.

HEART MOUNTAIN (2042 m) This mountain near Canmore was named for the heart-shaped strata at the crest of the mountain.

HEINSBURG This hamlet near Elk Point was named after its first postmaster, John Heins.

HEISLER Pop. 195. This village was named after Martin Heisler. The land for the village's townsite was purchased from Heisler. A post office opened here in 1915. Heisler is about 51 km northeast of Stettler.

HELL-ROARING CREEK This is a descriptive name for this turbulent creek that empties into Upper Waterton Lake. It is considered to be one of the most impressive sites in Waterton Lakes National Park.

HELL-ROARING FALLS Hell-Roaring Creek passes over these falls, located about 50 km south of Pincher Creek. (see Hell-Roaring Creek)

HELMET MOUNTAIN (2612 m) It is believed this mountain was named for its helmet-like shape. Helmet Mountain is about 41 km east-southeast of Jasper.

HEMARUKA The name of this hamlet is a combination of the first letters of the names belonging to CNR executive A.E. Warren's daughters, Helen, Margaret, Ruth and Kathleen. Hemaruka, about 60 km east-northeast of Hanna, was previously known as Zetland.

HESKETH This hamlet was named after Colonel J.A. Hesketh, an assistant divisional engineer of the Canadian Pacific Railway. Colonel Hesketh was also a graduate of the Royal Military College. Hesketh is near Drumheller.

HIGH LEVEL Pop. 3093. This is a relatively new town (incorporated in 1965) on the Mackenzie Highway. The name is descriptive of the nearby height of land that separates the Peace River and Hay River watersheds. High Level is about 250 km north of Peace River and is the most northerly bulk-grain shipping location in Canada. It is also a service centre for the oilfields at Rainbow Lake and Zama.

HIGH PRAIRIE Pop. 2907. This town about 100 km southeast of Peace River was named for the surrounding flat country. The High Prairie and District Museum highlights the history of the region and contains the Burley Collection of prehistoric artifacts. This archaeological collection contains two large macro-blades that may be between 8000 to 10,000 years old. These blades are the only ones of their size ever found in Canada.

HIGH ROCK RANGE This range about 70 km southwest of Turner Valley was named for the rocky features of its summit.

HILDA Pop. 45. This hamlet was named in 1910 after the daughter of local postmaster S. Koch. Hilda is about 63 km northeast of Medicine Hat.

HILL SPRING Pop. 206. This southern Alberta locality took its name from a spring on a nearby hill. Hill Spring is about 70 km southwest of Lethbridge.

HILLIARD This hamlet near Mundare was named for an early settler in the area, Hilliard McConkey.

HINES CREEK Pop. 437. This village near Fairview took its name from the nearby creek. It is believed the creek was named after an Anglican missionary who served at nearby Sandy Lake Mission from 1875 to 1888.

HINTON Pop. 9961. This town took its name from William Pitman Hinton. He was an executive with the Grand Trunk Pacific Railway. Hinton, a coal-mining and forestry community, is about 70 km northeast of Jasper.

HOBBEMA This hamlet was named after Meyndert Hobbema, a 17th-century Dutch landscape painter. This artist's paintings were favoured by Sir William Cornelius Van Horne, an early president of the Canadian Pacific Railway. (Van Horne was also an admirer of the works of Jean Francois Millet (see Millet).) Hobbema is near Wetaskiwin.

HOLDEN Pop. 397. This village about 45 km northeast of Camrose was named after James Bismark Holden. He served as grain elevator agent, a homestead inspector, businessman, Liberal member of the Alberta Legislature and mayor of Vegreville from 1912 to 1945. Holden was previously called Vermilion Valley.

HOLLEBEKE MOUNTAIN (2403 m) This mountain near Coleman was named after a village in Belgium where Canadian troops fought during World War I.

HORSESHOE CANYON This coulee near Drumheller was named for its shape.

HOWSE PEAK (3290 m) This mountain peak was named after Joseph Howse (1773–1852). He was a fur trader with

H

the Hudson's Bay Company and explored the Columbia and Kootenay rivers. Howse Peak is about 105 northwest of Banff.

HUGHENDEN Pop. 302. This village was named after Hughenden, Buckinghamshire, the English country estate of Benjamin Disraeli, the first Lord Beaconsfield and prime minister of Britain, off and on, through the 1850s, '60s and '70s. Hughenden is about 30 km southeast of Hardisty.

HUSSAR Pop. 157. This village near Drumheller was originally settled by a group of former German soldiers. They formed the German-Canadian Farming Company and bought 16 sections (41 square kilometres) of land from the Canadian Pacific Railway on which to build farms. Many in the group had been officers in the Kaiser's Hussars, an elite German cavalry unit. At the outbreak of World War I, most of these farmers tried to return to Germany to join the fighting, but they were prevented from doing so.

HUXLEY Pop. 77. This village near Trochu was named after Thomas Henry Huxley, an eminent British scientist. Huxley was famous for his support and defence of Darwin's theory on evolution.

HYLO This hamlet took its name from a term used in the game of faro. It is one of the oldest gambling card games and was played among workers laying the Alberta and Great Waterways Railway to this settlement, a village at the time. Hylo is near Lac La Biche.

HYTHE Pop. 712. This village was named after the English hometown of the community's first postmaster, Harry Hartley. Hythe is about 50 km west-northwest of Grande Prairie.

I

IDDESLEIGH This hamlet about 90 km northwest of Medicine Hat was named after Sir Walter Stafford Northcote, Earl of Iddesleigh. He served as governor of the Hudson's Bay Company from 1869 to 1874. He persuaded the HBC to take £300,000 in return for transferring most of the company's huge Rupert's Land territory to the Canadian government. A part of this vast territory is now the province of Alberta.

IMPERIAL MILLS This hamlet 30 km northeast of Lac La Biche took its name from a nearby sawmill owned by the Imperial Lumber Company. The community was previously known as Blefgen.

INDEFATIGABLE MOUNTAIN (2670 m) This mountain about 65 km west of Turner Valley was named after the HMS *Indefatigable*, a cruiser sunk during the 1916 Battle of Jutland.

INDIAN CABINS It is thought this hamlet took its name from the cabins in the area. Located on the Hay River, about 151 km north of High Level, this settlement was called *Tsentu*, meaning "dirty water" in old Slavey. It was so named because of the large amount of silt in the river.

INDIAN LOOKOUT (2591 m) This is believed to be a descriptive name. This mountain is located about 85 km north-northwest of Banff.

INDUS There are different versions of how this hamlet near Calgary was named. One theory relates to the hopes of Dr. J.M. Fulton, who saw industry taking hold in the community. "Industry" was shortened to "Indus." Another version has the hamlet being named after the Indus River and the Indus Valley, in India.

INNISFAIL Pop. 6773. There are different theories of how this town southwest of Red Deer was named. One account suggests that the name may have been proposed by a pioneer to honour the homeland of her grandmother, while another account has it that the name came from an Irish official of the Canadian Pacific Railway. *Innis Vail* is Gaelic for "Isle of Destiny."

INNISFREE Pop. 238. The village of Del Norte was renamed at the request of Sir Edmund Walker, president of the Canadian Bank of Commerce. The community reminded Walker of his summer residence, Innisfree, north of Toronto on Lake Simcoe, and he said he would establish a bank branch in the community if local residents changed its name to Innisfree. Townsfolk discussed the controversial idea and agreed to Walker's proposal. Innisfree is 37 km southeast of Vegreville.

INTERSECTION MOUNTAIN (2452 m) This mountain was named after the nearby intersection of the Continental Divide with the line of longitude at 120° West. It is here that the Alberta–BC boundary leaves the Continental Divide and instead goes directly northward along the longitude. Intersection Mountain is about 58 km west-southwest of Grande Cache.

IRMA Pop. 472. This village took its name from a daughter of William Wainwright, a senior executive with the Grand Trunk Pacific Railway. Irma is about 26 km northwest of Wainwright. Wainwright is named after Irma's father.

IRON SPRINGS This hamlet was named after mineral deposits found in the area. Iron Springs is approximately 25 km north-northeast of Lethbridge.

IRRICANA Pop. 962. This village took its name from a combination of the words "irrigation" and "canal." The Canadian government granted the land in the Bow Valley Irrigation Block to the CPR with the condition that the railway build an irrigation system using water from the Bow River. For various reasons, the irrigation project was never completed, and irrigation canals were never built near this centre. Irricana is about 42 km northeast of Calgary.

IRVINE Pop. less than 100. This hamlet near Medicine Hat was named for Colonel A. Irvine. Irvine was a commissioner of the North-West Mounted Police in the late 1800s and was an appointed member of the NWT government.

ISABELLE PEAK (2926 m) The origin of the name for this mountain peak is not certain. Isabelle Peak is about 35 km west-southwest of Banff.

ISLAY Pop. 158 This hamlet took its name from Islay, Scotland. The community was named by the Gilchrist family, the first settlers in the district. Islay is about 20 km east-northeast of Vermilion.

ISOLA PEAK (2499 m) The name of this mountain peak refers to its isolated location. This peak is located about 65 km west-northwest of Claresholm.

ITASKA BEACH Pop. 6. The name for this summer village on the north shore of Pigeon Lake comes from *itaskweyaw*, meaning "edge of the woods" in Cree. Itaska Beach is about 48 km west-northwest of Wetaskiwin.

J

JACKASS CANYON The origin of the name for this canyon about 48 km northwest of Calgary is uncertain. The name may refer to the mules used in the construction of the Canadian Pacific Railway.

JACKPINE MOUNTAIN (2650 m) This mountain took its name from the jackpine trees found in the area. Jackpine Mountain is about 113 km northwest of Jasper.

JANET The Canadian National Railway built a station here in 1912. The origin of the name for this Calgary area hamlet is not known.

JARROW This hamlet northwest of Wainwright took its name from a town in Durham, England. Jarrow, Alberta, was previously known as Jackson Coulee Post Office and Junkins.

JARVIE Pop. 105. This hamlet about 35 km northwest of Westlock was named after an employee of the Edmonton, Dunvegan and British Columbia Railway.

JASPER Pop. 4511. This town located in Jasper National Park was named after Jasper Hawes. He was in charge of the North West Company's trading post on Brûlé Lake in 1817. The post was later rebuilt as Jasper House near the present-day townsite of Jasper. It served for over 50 years as the main support station for a trade route over the mountains via Athabasca Pass to the West Coast. With the establishment of the Jasper Park Reserve in 1907, a new phase of development began for Jasper. Tourism followed, and the town also became a railway divisional point. In 2001, Jasper became a specialized municipality with power shared between Jasper's municipal government and Parks Canada Agency.

JEAN CÔTÉ This hamlet near Falher was named after Jean Léon Côté (1867–1924). Côté worked as a civil and mining engineer for the Canadian government and in private business. He served in the Alberta Legislature as a Liberal and was provincial secretary for three years. He was appointed to the Canadian Senate in 1923. (see Mount Côté)

JOSEPHBURG Pop. 144. This hamlet was named for Josefsberg, a village in Galicia, in the Austro-Hungarian Empire. The hamlet's pioneers originated in Josefsberg and nearby Bridgidau. The immigrants first settled in the Medicine Hat area, but after two successive crop failures, many of them moved north to today's Josephburg (near Edmonton). In the 1890s the Josefsberg Public School District was set up. Its secretary-treasurer spelled the name as "Josephburg," which became official.

JOUSSARD Pop. 225. There are a couple of versions of how this hamlet 75 km west of Slave Lake acquired its name. Perhaps it was named after an early settler in the area. On the other hand, perhaps it was named in honour of Bishop Henri Célestin Joussard, who served for 50 years in northern Alberta and the Northwest Territories.

JUMPINGPOUND MOUNTAIN (2225 m) This is a descriptive name for the steep banks where buffalo were hunted and killed by being stampeded over a cliff. Jumpingpound Mountain is about 55 km west of Calgary.

JUNCTION MOUNTAIN (2682 m) The name for this mountain refers to the point where two forks of the Sheep River meet. Junction Mountain is about 32 km west of Turner Valley.

JUTLAND MOUNTAIN (2408 m) This mountain 30 km northwest of Waterton Lakes National Park was named after the World War I Battle of Jutland. In this 1916 battle, the full British and Germans fleets met off the coast of Denmark to engage in battle. The British suffered greater losses, but the battle was seen as a draw between the two sides because the Germans had been unable to break the Allied naval blockade of their ports.

K

KAINAI NATION (BLOOD) INDIAN RESERVE #148.
This reserve about 40 km southeast of Pincher Creek is
the largest in Canada. It was established in 1883. A Blackfoot legend tells how the three nations of the old Blackfoot
Confederacy got their names. A mighty chief had three
sons. He named one Kainai, meaning "blood," another he
named Peaginour, meaning "wealth" and the third he did
not name immediately. Poor at hunting, the third son
appealed to his father, who with a charred stick blackened
the young man's feet and made him a great hunter. His
descendents are the Siksika (Blackfoot) Nation. The descendents of his two brothers are the Kainai (Blood) and the
Peigan.

KAKWA MOUNTAIN (2259 m) This mountain took its
name from the Cree word for "porcupine." Kakwa Mountain is about 65 km west-northwest of Grande Cache.

KANANASKIS RANGE This range about 80 km west of
Calgary was named after a Cree man, Kin-e-ah-kis, who,
according to legend, made a remarkable recovery after
taking an assailant's blow from an axe. The blow only
stunned him and was not fatal.

KANANASKIS VILLAGE This hamlet is about 17 km east of
Canmore. (see Kananaskis Range)

KAPASIWIN This summer village on Wabamun Lake, established in 1918, took its name from the translation of the
Cree word for "camp." It is the oldest summer village in
Alberta and was formerly called Wabamun Beach. Kapasiwin is about 55 km west of Edmonton.

KATAKA MOUNTAIN (2621 m) This is a descriptive name for this mountain, which has the appearance of a fort. *Kataka* is a Native word for "fort." The mountain is located near Jasper.

KATHLEEN This hamlet was named after a relative of W.R. Smith, a general manager of the Edmonton, Dunvegan and British Columbia Railway. Kathleen is about 35 km northwest of High Prairie.

KATHYRN This hamlet near Calgary took its name from Kathryn McKay, the daughter of a prominent landowner in the area. From the start, the name was misspelled.

KAUFMANN PEAKS (3109 m/3094 m) These peaks about 115 km northwest of Banff were named after Christian Kaufmann, a Swiss guide. Kaufmann was one of five prominent Swiss mountain guides brought to the Rockies by the Canadian Pacific Railway in 1905. The others were Edward, Ernest and Walter Feuz and Rudolph Aemmer.

KAVANAGH This hamlet south of Edmonton on the Calgary & Edmonton Railway was named in 1911 after Charles Edmund Kavanagh, superintendent of the railway mail service.

KEEPHILLS This hamlet was named after a town in Buckinghamshire, England. George Collins, the hamlet's first postmaster, suggested the name for this community, located about 45 km west of Edmonton.

KEG RIVER This locality, like the nearby Keg River railway point and the Keg River hamlet, was named after nearby Keg River. Dr. Mary Percy Jackson of the area maintained the name was a translation of the Cree place name that referred to a keg. It is located about 90 km south-southwest of High Level. (see Paddle Prairie Métis Settlement)

K

MORE ABOUT MARY PERCY…Lured by the idea of a romantic adventure in Canada's "wild west," a young British doctor set out in 1929 for northern Alberta. Dr. Mary Percy's trip across the Atlantic Ocean was likely easier and smoother than her long bone-shaking, mosquito-ridden trip by river barge and wagon to her new home in an isolated spot in the Peace River area. Here, the Alberta government, her employer, provided her with a home and hospital—a small shack with only the most basic medical supplies and no running water or electricity. This probably was not the romantic adventure she'd had in mind. Despite the hardships she faced, Percy fell in love with northern Alberta and provided medical care to the area. She later married farmer and rancher Frank Jackson and settled in Keg River, where she continued her practice. No longer employed by the provincial government, the doctor was often paid in blueberries, moccasins and moosemeat. Mary Percy Jackson provided medical care to the area until her retirement in 1974. She received many awards for her service, including the Centennial Medal of Canada.

KELSEY Pop. 19. This hamlet was named after a homesteader in the district, Moses S. Kelsey. Kelsey is about 27 km southeast of Camrose.

KEOMA The name for this hamlet comes from a Native word meaning "far away." Keoma was settled in the early 1900s and is not far away from Calgary.

KERENSKY This locality near Redwater was named after Aleksandr Fedorovich Kerensky, the provisional president of Russia after the abdication of Czar Nicholas II. Kerensky led the turbulent country for a few months until the Bolshevik "October Revolution" in November 1917.

KICKING HORSE PASS (1642 m) This pass took its name from an incident involving Sir James Hector and a horse. While attempting to catch his runaway pack horse, Sir James was kicked by the beast. Hector, surgeon and geologist of the Palliser Expedition, was not seriously hurt, and the expedition chose this name for the pass. Kicking Horse Pass, about 60 km northwest of Banff, carries the CPR transcontinental line and the Trans-Canada Highway. (see Yellowhead Pass)

MORE ABOUT JAMES HECTOR… *James Hector was a talented man whose skills went far beyond his training as a medical doctor. His special interest in geology, natural history and scientific botany made him a good choice for the famed Palliser Expedition, which explored much of western Canada. Among his many contributions, Hector recognized three topographic levels in the plains, produced many diagrams of the geology of the area, described the general structure of the Rockies and discovered the Continental Divide on the Kicking Horse Pass. After his work with the Palliser Expedition from 1857 to 1860, Hector became director of the geological survey for New Zealand. He returned to Canada for a short visit in 1903 and died in New Zealand four years later at the age of 73.*

K

KILLAM Pop. 1048. This town was named after A.C. Killam, the first chairman of the Board of Railway Commissioners. The town honoured the first eight governors general of Canada by naming some of its streets and avenues after the Queen's representative in Canada, namely: Stanley, Minto, Dufferin, Monck, Aberdeen, Lansdowne, Lorne and Lisgar. Killam is about 70 km east-southeast of Camrose.

KIMBALL This hamlet was named after Herber C. Kimball, whose grandsons were early settlers in the area. The hamlet of Kimball, formerly known as Colles, is located about 71 km southwest of Lethbridge.

KINGMAN Pop. 93. This hamlet near Camrose was named after its first postmaster, F.W. Kingsbury. The plan was to call the community Kingsbury, but as that name had already been taken by another settlement, a modification was required.

KINSELLA This hamlet was named in 1910 after the private secretary of a Grand Trunk Pacific Railway vice-president. Kinsella is about 30 km southeast of Viking.

KINUSO Pop. 258. This village took its name from the Cree word for "fish" and likely reflects the number of fish in the nearby lake. Kinuso is about 40 km west of Slave Lake.

KIPP This locality near Lethbridge was named after Fort Kipp, a whiskey-trading fort built in 1870. The post's founder Joseph Kipp, a U.S. citizen, sold whiskey to Natives in exchange for furs. He was only in business there a few years before the NWMP shut him down. Today's Kipp is several kilometres east of the original post that was built where the Belly River flows into the Oldman.

K

KIRKCALDY This hamlet was named after Kirkcaldy, Fife, Scotland. Kirkcaldy is about 87 km southeast of Calgary.

KIRRIEMUIR This hamlet about 47 km south of Provost was named after a Scottish community. "Kirriemuir" comes from the Gaelic *ceathramh mor*, meaning "big quarter."

KITSCOTY Pop. 672. This village took its name from a town in Kent, England. The English town's name comes from "Kit's Coty House," meaning "the tomb in the woods." Kit's Coty House is a doleman—a prehistoric monument that is thought to have been used a a tomb and consists of two or more large upright stones supporting a horizontal stone slab.

KNIFE MOUNTAIN (2057 m) Knife Mountain is located near Grande Cache. The origin of the name is not certain.

KOOTENAY PLAINS These plains about 120 km northwest of Banff are about 12 km long and 4 km wide. They were the place where, in the mid-1800s, Kootenay Natives of Interior BC bartered their furs to traders from forts on the Saskatchewan River.

KRAKOW This locality 10 km south of Wostok was named sometime around 1900 after an ancient Polish city, at the time a part of the Austro-Hungarian Empire. Galician settlers from the city of Krakow named this locality.

K

L

LA COULOTTE PEAK (2387/2425 m) This peak about 35 km northwest of Waterton Lakes National Park was named after a place near Lens, France.

LA CRÈCHE MOUNTAIN (2314 m) This mountain, at the time of its naming in 1925, was being used by young goats to practise their climbing. La Crèche Mountain is located about 57 km west-northwest of Grande Cache.

LA CRÈTE This hamlet took its name from a nearby ridge that resembles a rooster's comb (*la crête* in French). The local Rivard brothers chose this name. *Crête* is also the French word for "ridge" or "crest." La Crête is about 56 km southwest of High Level.

LA GLACE This hamlet was named after Charles La Glace, chief of the Beaver Natives and a settler in the area. He gained respect from white settlers and the members of his tribe for avoiding violence despite the many conflicts between white settlers and his tribe.

LABYRINTH MOUNTAIN (2118 m) This mountain was named for its resemblance to a labyrinth. Labyrinth Mountain is located about 70 km north of Canmore.

LAC LA BICHE Pop. 2611. This town sits 170 km northeast of Edmonton on the shores of a lake named Lac La Biche. This lake was named after the deer in the area. Through the 1800s, *biche* was the word used by French-Canadian fur traders for "elk" and "deer." A literal translation of the town's name is "lake of the red doe." The town of Lac La Biche has a long history. Fur company posts were established here as early as the 1790s. At nearby "Portage la

Biche," travellers crossed a thin headland between Beaver Lake and Lac La Biche. Beaver Lake drains into the Beaver River, which flows into the Saskatchewan River and the Hudson Bay, while water from Lac La Biche flows into the Athabasca/Mackenzie waterway. Thus Lac La Biche was important for travel and trade into the Far North. Lac La Biche is about 80 km east of Athabasca.

MORE ABOUT LAC LA BICHE...*David Thompson built the first trading post in the Lac La Biche area. Born in England in 1770, Thompson was apprenticed to the Hudson's Bay Company at age 14. Thompson was an explorer, fur trader, surveyor and mapmaker. He devoted most of his life to geography and mapmaking. Thompson mapped much of the vast western area that has become part of Canada. In addition to mapping the Prairies, Thompson explored west of the Rockies, including the Columbia River basin. He reached the Pacific Ocean in 1811. The following year he returned to Williamstown (in present-day Ontario) and continued working as a surveyor and map-maker. Thompson has been recognized as one of the world's top map-makers.*

LAC LA BICHE MISSION This abandoned mission 11 km south of Lac La Biche is a National Historic Site. The mission was established in 1855 by Oblate missionaries, and the historic site includes a convent, a rectory and a church.

LACOMBE Pop. 8517. This town near Red Deer was named after Father Albert Lacombe. He was a Roman Catholic missionary of the Oblates of Mary Immaculate. Born in Québec, Father Lacombe was ordained a priest in 1849. He moved to HBC-held Rupert's Land (western Canada) where he worked with the Red River Métis. In 1851, he moved to what would be Alberta and established a mission at St. Albert, near Edmonton. For 60 years he ministered to and worked with the Prairie Natives. (see St. Albert)

LAFOND This hamlet was named after C.B. Lafond, a homesteader who came to this area from Québec in the early 1900s. Lafond is near St. Paul.

LAKE ATHABASCA (see Athabasca River)

LAKE LOUISE Nestled in the Rocky Mountains, this hamlet is one of the most beautiful resorts—anywhere. The nearby lake itself is described as one of the seven natural wonders of the world. This hamlet, formerly known as Holt City and as Laggan, was named in 1914 in honour of Princess Louise Caroline Alberta. Lake Louise is 60 km northwest of Banff.

LAKE MINNEWANKA This lake near Banff has a Native name that translates as "Lake of the Evil Water-Spirit" or "Devil's Lake." According to legend, a Native man saw a fish in the lake that was as long as the lake itself.

L

LAKEVIEW Pop. 15. This summer village about 51 km northeast of Drayton Valley has a descriptive name.

LAKE VIEW RIDGE This ridge in Waterton Lakes National Park was named for its commanding view of the park.

LAMONT Pop. 1581. This town was named in 1906 after Mr. Justice Lamont of the Supreme Court of Canada. Before being appointed to the Supreme Court, Justice Lamont practised law and served as a MP and a Saskatchewan MLA (serving as the province's first attorney general). He also served as a Saskatchewan Supreme Court judge.

LANGDON Pop. 390. This hamlet near Calgary was named after R.B. Langdon of the construction firm Langdon and Shepard, contractors who built the Canadian Pacific Railway line in the district. The nearby hamlet of Shepard was named at the same time.

LAVOY This village near Vegreville took its name from Joseph Lavoy. He was an early settler. Lavoy was previously known as Dinwoodie.

LEAH PEAK (2801 m) This mountain peak took its name from the wife of Stoney Chief Samson Beaver. Leah Peak is about 40 km southeast of Jasper.

LEATHER PEAK (2286 m) This mountain peak west of Jasper took its name from the many leather skins carried by fur traders through nearby Yellowhead Pass, which was once known as Leather Pass.

LEAVITT This hamlet about 80 km southwest of Lethbridge was named after T.R. Leavitt, an early settler in the area.

LECTERN PEAK (2772 m) This mountain resembles a church lectern. Lectern Peak is near Jasper.

LEDUC Pop. 14,540. This city near Edmonton was named in honour of Father Hippolyte Leduc, of the Oblates of Mary Immaculate. Father Leduc came to the Edmonton area in 1867 and served in various missions in western Canada. Around 1890, Leduc was the site of a telegraph office on the telegraph line from Fort Garry. The community gained fame in 1947 as an oil centre when Imperial Leduc No. 1 started up. This was the beginning of the Edmonton area oil boom. Leduc was made a village in 1899, a town in 1906 and a city in 1983.

LEGAL Pop. 1095. This village was named in honour of Emile Joseph Légal, the first Roman Catholic archbishop of Edmonton, in 1912. As an Oblate, Archbishop Légal spent many years in the missionary field and authored *Short Sketches of the History of the Catholic Churches and Missions in Central Alberta.*

LESLIEVILLE Pop. 147. This hamlet was named after Leslie Reilly, a settler in the area. Leslieville is about 25 km east of Rocky Mountain House.

LESSER SLAVE LAKE This lake near High Prairie took its name from the Cree name for the lake. Cree coming into the area encountered (and pushed out) Natives of a different tribe, perhaps Beaver or Blackfoot, who were already established there. The Cree word for "stranger" was translated to mean "slave," giving the lake the English place name in use today. The term "Lesser" distinguishes it from the Great Slave Lake in the Northwest Territories.

LETHBRIDGE Pop. 78,713. This city was named after William Lethbridge. Lethbridge, a partner in the London bookstore W.H. Smith and Sons, was the first president of the North Western Coal and Navigation Company, Limited. The scope of the coal-mining operations on the banks of the Oldman River influenced the original name of this community. Coalhurst and Coal Banks were names in common usage in the area. But in 1882, Coal Banks was renamed "Lethbridge." There was already a Lethbridge in Ontario, so the postal authorities did not give official recognition to the name. However, they changed their minds when three years later the name Lethbridge was still commonly used in the southern Alberta community. The officials replaced both Coal Banks and Coalhurst with Lethbridge. The Blackfoot knew the area as *siko-ko-toki*, meaning "black rocks." It is estimated that some 500 generations of Blackfoot lived in the Lethbridge area before recorded history. (see Coalhurst)

LEYLAND MOUNTAIN (2545 m) This mountain was named after F.W. Leyland, an executive of the Mountain Park Coal Company. Leyland Mountain is about 90 km southwest of Edson.

LICK PEAK (2877 m) This peak took its name from a nearby salt deposit where wild animals lick up salt. Lick Peak is located about 50 km south-southeast of Jasper.

LINDBERGH This hamlet was named in honour of Charles Lindbergh, a U.S. adventurer and pilot who in 1927 was the first to fly solo from New York City to Paris, France. Lindbergh is near Elk Point.

LINDEN Pop. 590. It is not certain why this name was chosen for this village near Three Hills. It may have been named after an early settler in the area.

LINEHAM CREEK This creek near Turner Valley was named after John Lineham. He was a leading pioneer in the area, having business interests in lumber, oil, cattle and horses. Lineham also served as a representative in the Legislative Assembly of the North-West Territories.

LISBURN It is believed this hamlet was named after a town in Antrim, Ireland (now Northern Ireland). Lisburn, near Mayerthorpe, was formerly known as Merebeck.

LISTENING MOUNTAIN (3149 m) This name refers to two ear-like features on this mountain. Listening Mountain is 75 km southeast of Jasper.

LITTLE SMOKY This hamlet was named after the Little Smoky River, which got its name from the smoke caused by nearby coal beds igniting and smoldering, sometimes for years, producing clouds of smoke that hang in the air. Little Smoky is near High Prairie and flows into the Smoky River.

LIVINGSTONE RANGE This range near Blairmore was named after Dr. David Livingstone. (see Mount Livingstone)

LLOYDMINSTER Pop. 11,317. This city, incorporated in 1958, is often called Border City, because it is split by the Alberta–Saskatchewan border. It was named after George Exton Lloyd, who was chaplain to this all-British colony and later became the Anglican bishop for Saskatchewan. *Lloydminster* means "Lloyd's monastery," as *minster* is the

Old English word for "monastery." The city of Lloydminster is exceptional in that it is recognized by the governments of both Alberta and Saskatchewan.

LODGEPOLE This hamlet was named after the lodgepole pine in the area. Lodgepole is near Drayton Valley.

LOGAN RIDGE This ridge was named after a settler in the area. Logan Ridge is located about 30 km west of Calgary.

LOMOND Pop. 170. Perhaps this village took its name from Loch Lomond, Scotland. On the other hand, perhaps Lomond was named after Lomond Dugal McCarthy, an early homesteader in the area. Lomond is about 70 km north-northeast of Lethbridge.

LONE MOUNTAIN (2423 m) This mountain on the western boundary of Waterton Lakes National Park took its name from its isolated location.

LONE PINE This locality was first established as a post office in 1930, and it presumably took its name from the solitary pine tree in the area. Lone Pine is 40 km north of Mayerthorpe.

LONG LAKE PROVINCIAL PARK This is a descriptive name referring to the long, narrow shape of the park's lake. Long Lake Provincial Park is located south of Boyle.

LONGVIEW Pop. 303. This village was named after Thomas Long, an early settler in the area. This place name refers to the long view from a nearby hill once used as a lookout. Longview is near Turner Valley.

LOOP RIDGE (2003 m) This mountain near Coleman took its name from a nearby loop of railway track.

LOST MOUNTAIN (2512 m) This descriptive name refers to the mountain's isolated position. Lost Mountain is near Waterton Lakes National Park.

LOUGHEED Pop. 253. This village near Sedgewick was named in honour of Sir James Alexander Lougheed, K.C.M.G. who practised law in Toronto and Calgary. He was legal counsel for the Canadian Pacific Railway and a director of Canada Life Assurance Company. Lougheed was appointed to the Senate in 1889 and served as Conservative leader there from 1906 to 1921, as well as serving in the federal cabinet. Mount Loughheed is also named after him. His grandson Peter served as premier of Alberta from 1971 to 1985.

MORE ABOUT PETER LOUGHEED... *In six short years, Peter Lougheed took the Alberta Progressive Conservative party from almost a standing start to form the provincial government in 1971. His election victory brought to an end 36 years of Social Credit government in the province. Edgar Peter Lougheed was born in 1928 into one of Calgary's leading families. The Lougheeds, like many other prairie families, had been hit hard by the Depression, and young Peter did much to restore the family's prominence before becoming involved in politics. Although he held and excelled at senior positions within the Mannix Corporation, Peter Lougheed had a passion for politics. He left his mark by pushing for a stronger voice for the province in national decision-making. Consistently winning large majorities at the polls, Premier Lougheed dominated provincial politics in much the same manner as his Social Credit predecessors.*

L

LOUSANA William H. Biggs wanted to name this hamlet near Red Deer after his hometown. This settler from Louisiana, Missouri, donated land for the new townsite. His suggestion that the community take the name Louisiana was not accepted by postal authorities in Ottawa. They insisted that it be shortened to Lousana to avoid confusion among the public.

LOYALIST Many communities in Alberta took names commemorating the coronation of King George V on June 22, 1911. These communities include Consort, Veteran, Throne, Coronation and Loyalist. The locality of Loyalist is about 35 km east-southeast of Coronation.

LUCERNE PEAK (2316 m) This mountain took its name from Lucerne Lake and Lucerne Canton, both in Switzerland. Lucerne Peak is located about 34 km west of Jasper.

LUNDBRECK Pop. 234. This hamlet name is a combination of the names of the owners of the Breckenridge & Lund Coal Company, which ran collieries and sawmills at this location. This community is situated near Cowley and at the mouth of the Crowsnest Pass.

LUSCAR MOUNTAIN (2591 m) This mountain took its name from Luscar, Fifeshire, Scotland. Luscar Mountain is located about 90 km southwest of Edson.

L

LYALTA This hamlet's name is a compound of Lyall and Alberta. It was suggested by A. Harry Parsons of Lyall Trading Company. Lyalta is about 28 km east of Calgary.

LYCHNIS MOUNTAIN (2819 m) This mountain took its name from the wildflower that is also known as alpine campion. Lychnis Mountain is about 44 km northwest of Banff.

LYNX MOUNTAIN (3192 m) This mountain took its name from a dead lynx found in the vicinity. Lynx Mountain is about 70 km west-northwest of Jasper.

M

MA-ME-O BEACH Pop. 81. This summer village took its name from the Cree word *mee-mee-o*, which roughly translates as "place of lots of shorebirds" or as "white pigeon." Ma-Me-O Beach is about 40 km west of Wetaskiwin.

MACKAY This hamlet about 130 km west of Edmonton just off the Yellowhead Highway was named after railway contractor J.C. MacKay. The Canadian Northern Railway opened a station in MacKay in 1911.

MACKENZIE HIGHWAY The Mackenzie Highway, established in 1945, runs about 1200 km from the Alberta town of Peace River, past Great Slave Lake, to Wrigley, NWT, on the Mackenzie River.

MADDEN This hamlet was named after prominent pioneer rancher Bernard "Barney" Madden. Madden is about 46 km north-northwest of Calgary.

MAGNOLIA BRIDGE This hamlet northwest of Stony Plain was named after Magnolia Bluffs in Washington State. Local residents noted the resemblance between the two locations.

MAGRATH Pop. 1867. This town south of Lethbridge was named after Charles A. Magrath. He was a local businessman and politician. In the late 1800s, he served as a member of the North-West Territorial government and, from 1908 to 1911, as a Member of Parliament for Medicine Hat. He also served as a Canadian member of the International Joint Commission from 1911 to 1936.

MAJESTIC MOUNTAIN (3086 m) This mountain was named for its majestic presence. Majestic Mountain is the highest peak in its range and is located near Jasper.

MALIGNE LAKE Maligne Lake is located about 34 km southeast of Jasper. This lake took its name from the French word *maligne*, meaning "bad." Maligne River, which drains Maligne Lake, perhaps earned this derogatory name because of its speed. Maligne Lake was first seen by white men (surveyor Henry MacLeod) in 1875, but was still a secluded spot in the early 1900s, its location a Native secret. (see Mount Paul) (see Valad Peak)

MALIGNE MOUNTAIN (3150 m) Mary Schäffer named this mountain after nearby Maligne Lake during her 1911 expedition to the lake. Jack Unwin, of Mount Unwin fame, assisted with the expedition. Maligne Mountain is located about 50 km southeast of Jasper. (see Maligne Lake)

MALLAIG Pop. 183. This hamlet near St. Paul was named after a town in Inverness-shire, Scotland.

MALLARD PEAK (2835 m) The name for this mountain is derived from its shape, which is similar to that of a mallard duck. Mallard Peak is about 47 km south-southwest of Jasper.

MANNING Pop. 1295. This town was named after Ernest C. Manning. He was a radio evangelist, politician and the longest-serving premier of Alberta. Manning started his long career as a student of William Aberhart at the Calgary Prophetic Bible Institute. Manning is located 73 km northwest of Peace River.

MORE ABOUT ERNEST MANNING...*The political career of Ernest Charles Manning began with the election of Aberhart's Social Credit government. In 1935, Manning became Canada's youngest cabinet minister at the age of 26. Later, on the death of Premier Aberhart in 1943, Manning was the unanimous choice of the Social Credit caucus to lead the party and the province as premier.*

M

He was premier for 25 years and won some elections with large majorities. He was premier at a time when the province was shifting from a farm-based economy to one incorporating the energy sector, which became important after the discovery of the Leduc oilfield in 1947. In addition to being a deft politician who was able to keep his finger on the "pulse" of the people, Manning faithfully kept up his weekly radio program "Canada's National Back to the Bible Hour." Unlike Aberhart, Manning did not blend his political philosophy with his religious messages, but there is little doubt this high profile program helped maintain his political base. Manning resigned as premier in 1968. After politics, he took positions on various corporate boards, served in the Senate from 1970 to 1983 and was made a Companion of the Order of Canada.

MANOLA This hamlet near Barrhead was named for one of the daughters of James Albert McPhee, an early pioneer. The post office opened here in 1907.

MANNVILLE Pop. 758. This village near Vermilion was named in honour of Sir Donald Mann. Mann and Sir William Mackenzie were founders and senior executives of Canadian Northern Railway. They were knighted in 1911. Their railways suffered during World War I and were taken over by the federal government in the 1920s to form the Canadian National Railway.

MANX PEAK (3044 m) This name describes the shape of this mountain, which looks like the coat of arms for the Isle of Man. The word Manx means "of or relating to the Isle of Man." Manx Peak is close to Jasper.

MANYBERRIES The name for this hamlet is derived from the Blackfoot place name *akoniskway*, meaning "many berries." The Native place name refers to the different types of wild berries found in the area. These include chokecherries and saskatoons, with which Natives made

M

pemmican. Manyberries is about 72 km south of Medicine Hat.

MARKERVILLE Pop. 50. This hamlet, an Icelandic Canadian settlement, was named after C.P. Marker, a dairy commissioner for the North-West Territories and Alberta. The first post office in the area took its name from Tindastoll (a mountain in Iceland), showing the prevalence of Icelandic settlement in the area. In 1889, Icelandic poet Stephán G. Stephansson moved to this area near Innisfail.

MORE ABOUT STEPHÁN STEPHANSSON... *Stephán Stephansson was born in 1853 in Iceland. He and his family immigrated to the United States in 1873, but in 1889 he, by then with a family of his own, moved to Canada. He took up homesteading in the Markerville area, at that time in the North-West Territories. Largely self-educated, Stephansson began writing poetry at the age of 15. By the early 1900s, he was regarded as the leading Icelandic poet of the last 600 years. Stephansson was known for his pacifism and his interest in women's rights. He took an active role in the cultural life of Icelandic Canadians. Although he had a deep affection for his homeland, Stephansson considered himself a Canadian, and his love for Alberta was reflected in his poems.*

MARLBORO Pop. 175. This hamlet about 170 km west of Edmonton took its name from the area's deposits of marl, a substance used to make cement. A cement plant belonging to the Edmonton Portland Cement Company was built here in 1911 and went into operation in 1913. The plant only operated for one year before the World War I recession forced it to close. It reopened in 1917 on a seasonal basis and operated through the 1920s. By 1980 the mouldering remains of the plant buildings topped by a tall industrial smokestack were all that remained.

MARMOT MOUNTAIN (2608 m) This mountain near Jasper took its name from the marmots found in the area. The marmot is a burrowing rodent and is known for its shrill call.

MARVEL PEAK (2713 m) This name is descriptive of the beauty of this peak. It is located 105 km west of Calgary.

MARWAYNE Pop. 449. This village was named by Fred Marfleet, an early settler in the district. The name is a combination of the first part of his surname and the name of Marfleet's old home in England, Wainfleet (occasionally spelled Wayneflete). Marwayne is near Lloydminster.

MASTODON MOUNTAIN (2987 m) This is a descriptive name for this mountain, which is said to resemble the shape of a mastodon (an extinct elephant-like animal). Mastodon Mountain is about 35 km southwest of Jasper.

MAYERTHORPE Pop. 1669. This town took its name from a combination of the names of two early settlers in the area. It was named after R.I. Mayer, its first postmaster, and one Mr. Thorpe. Mayerthorpe is about 115 km west-northwest of Edmonton.

MAZEPPA This locality about 35 km southeast of Calgary was named after the hero of Lord Byron's poem "Mazeppa", a Cossack hetman (meaning commander) by that name. In 1912, the Canadian Pacific Railway opened a station in this community.

MCLAUGHLIN This hamlet near Lloydminster was named after John and Thomas McLaughlin, early settlers in the district.

MCLENNAN Pop. 957. This town was incorporated in 1948 and was named after Dr. J.K. McLennan, a senior official with the Edmonton, Dunvegan and British Columbia Railway. McLennan is about 135 km northeast of Grande Prairie.

M

MORE ABOUT MCLENNAN... *Situated on Kimiwan Lake, McLennan is known as the Bird Capital of Canada. The Mississippi, Pacific and Central Migration Paths converge here, and an estimated 250,000 waterfowl and 27,000 shorebirds pass through McLennan each year. Sometimes 200 different species can be sighted.*

MEANOOK This hamlet near Athabasca took its name from the Cree word for "good camping place."

MEDICINE HAT Pop. 56,048. The name for this city comes from a translation of the Blackfoot place name *saamis*, meaning "the headdress of a medicine man." According to legend, during a battle between Native nations, a Cree medicine man lost his war bonnet in the nearby South Saskatchewan River while fleeing from Blackfoot attackers. Another version of how Medicine Hat received its name tells of a Native chief who had a vision of a man rising from the South Saskatchewan River wearing the hat of a medicine man. Medicine Hat is a service centre for the ranching and farming region and is also a prosperous industrial city. It is about 150 km east-northeast of Lethbridge.

MEDICINE LODGE COULEE This coulee about 58 km southeast of Medicine Hat was a location for Native spiritual ceremonies. Week-long ceremonial Sun Dances were often held here.

MEETING CREEK This hamlet near Bashaw was named for its closeness to the creek of the same name. The creek was so named because Cree from the north and Blackfoot from the south often met here during buffalo hunts.

MEKASTOE This former locality west of Lethbridge was named after Mekasto (Red Crow), a chief of the southern Blood tribe. Red Crow and other leaders of the Blackfoot Confederacy, such as Chief Crowfoot, signed Treaty 7 in 1877. In this treaty, the Natives gave up their sovereignty over the land in exchange for yearly cash payments, access to education and other benefits, while maintaining their traditional hunting and fishing rights.

METISKOW This hamlet took its name from the Cree place name *metosi skaw*, meaning "many trees." Metiskow is about 25 km west-northwest of Provost.

MIDWAY PEAK (2871 m) This is a descriptive name for this mountain located midway between Stairway Peak and Mount Synge. Midway Peak is about 100 km northwest of Banff.

MILK RIVER Pop. 929. This town about 110 km south of Medicine Hat took its name from the Milk River, which has water that is "milky" in colour. The Milk River is the only river in Alberta whose waters flow into the Gulf of Mexico. Milk River flows into the Missouri, which flows into the Mississippi.

MILL CREEK This creek flowing through Edmonton was named for a gristmill nearby. The mill was operated by HBC's William Bird from 1871 to 1874. (A creek west of Pincher Creek also carries this name because of a sawmill that operated on its banks from 1880 to about 1930.)

MILLET Pop. 1894. There are different versions of how this town near Wetaskiwin was named. Although "millet" is the name for a type of grain, it seems that the centre was named after an individual. Perhaps it was named after the famous French painter Jean François Millet (1815–75). Sir William Cornelius Van Horne, an early president of the CPR, was a great admirer of the works of Millet, as well as those of Meyndert Hobbema (see Hobbema). It is thought that Van Horne named this community after the artist. Millet's paintings of the "The Angelus" and "The Man with a Hoe" are well known. Perhaps, though, the town was named after a local fur buyer, August Millet. The Calgary & Edmonton Railway gave Father Lacombe the opportunity to name the railway's sidings, which in many cases quickly grew into settlements and towns. It is possible Father Lacombe named this siding after his old travelling companion.

MILLICENT The Fourth Duke of Sutherland had large land-holdings in this part of southern Alberta. His wife, Lady Millicent Fanny St. Claire-Erskine, the Fourth Duchess of Sutherland, may be the namesake for this hamlet. Or, it could have been named after their daughter, Rosemary Millicent, who was the namesake of the hamlet of Rosemary. The hamlet of Millicent is about 104 km northwest of Medicine Hat. (see Erskine)

MILO Pop. 121. This village was named after its early postmaster, Milo Munroe. Milo is located about 90 km southeast of Calgary.

MINBURN Pop. 95. This village took its name from the name of Ottawa writer Mina Burns, who wrote articles on western Canada. Minburn is about 34 km west of Vermilion.

MIRROR Pop. 487. This village was named after the *Daily Mirror* of London, England. The newspaper informed its readers of the opportunities in this part of the province. Mirror is near Bashaw.

MISSION BEACH This hamlet on the north shore of Pigeon Lake was named for its proximity to the Rundle Mission, established in 1847.

MITRE, THE (2886 m) This mountain resembles a bishop's mitre. The Mitre is about 55 km west-northwest of Banff.

MOLAR MOUNTAIN (3022 m) This is a descriptive name for this tooth-shaped mountain. Molar Mountain is located about 65 km northwest of Banff.

MONARCH MOUNTAIN (2896 m) The origin of the name for this mountain is not certain. Monarch Mountain is located about 27 km northwest of Jasper.

MONARCH This hamlet west of Lethbridge came into being with the 1908 rerouting of the Canadian Pacific Railway in the Lethbridge area. Before 1908, the CPR line followed a circuitous route in the area, using many small bridges, winding through coulees and negotiating various grades in the process. This was perhaps an interesting trip for poets or those wanting a chance to view the subtle scenery of the Prairies, but engineers thought there had to be a more efficient way of making the journey. The route was changed with the building of two long steel bridges, one at Lethbridge and one a little west, allowing a direct route for the railway. A townsite was established at the second bridge. This became Monarch. The name was chosen to reflect the hopes and aspirations of the area's settlers.

MONCHY MOUNTAIN (3210 m) This mountain was named after a village in France captured by British troops in the final offensive of World War I. Monchy Mountain is about 120 km southeast of Jasper.

MONITOR This hamlet took its name from a community in England. Monitor, previously known as Sounding Lake, is about 46 km south-southwest of Provost.

MONKHEAD MOUNTAIN (3211 m) This name is descriptive of this mountain located about 90 km west of Nordegg.

MONS PEAK (3083 m) This mountain was named after the Belgian town that was the scene of the British Expeditionary Force's first battle during World War I. Mons Peak is about 125 km northeast of Banff.

MORECAMBE This hamlet near Two Hills took its name from the Morecambe Bay in England.

M

MORINVILLE Pop. 6226. This town was founded in 1891 by Abbé Jean-Baptiste Morin (1852–1911). He wrote the important pamphlet *Le Nord-ouest Canadien et ses Resources Agricoles* and four books, and he founded several French-speaking settlements in Alberta. He is credited with bringing 483 families to Alberta.

MORLEY This locality was named after Reverend Dr. Morley Punshon, a prominent Methodist minister. After getting Rev. Punshon's approval, Rev. George McDougall opened a mission here. Morley is about 60 km northwest of Calgary.

MORRIN Pop. 275. It is likely this village was named after the engineer who drove the first train into the community. Morrin is about 36 km east of Three Hills.

MORRO PEAK (1678 m) This name refers to the shape of this peak located near Jasper. *Morro* is the Spanish word for "round hill."

MOUNT ALBERTA (3619 m) This mountain 77 km southeast of Jasper was named after Princess Louise Caroline Alberta, who was also the namesake of the province.

MOUNT ALLAN (2789 m) This mountain about 80 km west of Calgary was named in 1948 after Dr. J.A. Allan (1884–1955). Dr. Allan founded the Department of Geology at the University of Alberta. He also made a major contribution to surveying Alberta's coal resources.

MOUNT ALLEN (3310 m) The name for this mountain about 50 km northwest of Banff is derived from Samuel Evan S. Allen (1874–1945). Originally from Philadelphia, he was a pioneer climber in the Rockies and named the Valley of the Ten Peaks.

MOUNT ALLENBY (2995 m) This mountain was named after Field Marshal Viscount Edmund Henry Hynman

Allenby (1861–1936). Viscount Allenby was commander of the British Army in Palestine during World War I. Mount Allenby is about 100 km west of Calgary.

MOUNT AMERY (3329 m) This mountain 120 km southeast of Jasper took its name from Leopold Charles Maurice Stennett Amery (1873–1955). He was a member of the British House of Lords and an avid mountaineer. Amery climbed the peak in 1929.

MOUNT ANDROMEDA (2806 m) The name for this mountain is from Greek mythology. Andromeda was the wife of Perseus and daughter of Cassiopeia and King Cepheus. Mount Andromeda is about 95 km southeast of Jasper.

MOUNT ARÊTE (2990 m) This name describes the sharp-crested, or knife-edged, ridge. Mount Arête is about 90 km southeast of Jasper.

MOUNT ARETHUSA (2912 m) This mountain took its name from a British cruiser sunk by a mine during World War I. Mount Arethusa is 49 km west of Turner Valley.

MOUNT ARMSTRONG (2823 m) This mountain 49 km southwest of Turner Valley was named in honour of a member of the Surveyor General's staff, J.D. Armstrong, who was killed in action in World War I.

MOUNT ASSINIBOINE (3618 m) George Mercer Dawson, director of the Geological Survey of Canada from 1895 to 1901, named this mountain after the Assiniboine Sioux. *Assiniboine* is the Cree word for "stoney." The name was given to these people because of their way of cooking—they added hot stones to animal-hide bowls of water-immersed food. Mount Assiniboine is about 105 km west of Calgary.

MOUNT ATHABASCA (3491 m) Mount Athabasca is located 95 km south of Jasper. (see Athabasca River)

M

MOUNT AVENS (2970 m) This mountain was named after a type of wildflower common to the area. Mount Avens is about 40 km northwest of Banff.

MOUNT AYLMER (3162 m) This mountain was named by J.J. McArthur, a Dominion Lands surveyor. He named the mountain after his hometown of Aylmer, Québec. Mount Aylmer is near Banff.

MOUNT AZTEC (2816 m) The name for this mountain refers to a zigzag of red rock near its summit. Zigzag symbols similar to it were a favourite of the Aztecs. Mount Aztec is about 90 km northwest of Jasper.

MOUNT BABEL (3101 m) This mountain about 45 km west-northwest of Banff is said to resemble a nearby mountain named Tower of Babel.

MOUNT BACKUS (1815 m) This mountain was named after an area homesteader. Mount Backus is near Pincher Creek.

MOUNT BAKER (3172 m) This mountain was named in 1898 after G.P. Baker. He was a member in the Alpine Club of London, England. Mount Baker is 90 km northwest of Banff.

MOUNT BALCARRES (2897 m) This mountain took its name from Balcarres, Scotland, the home of Sir Coutts Lindsay, a friend of the western Canadian explorer Earl of Southesk. Mount Balcarres is about 50 km east-southeast of Jasper. (see Mount Balinhard) (see Mount Lindsay)

MOUNT BALDY (2192 m) This is a descriptive name for the bare top of the mountain. Mount Baldy is near Canmore.

MOUNT BALFOUR (3272 m) Sir James Hector of the Palliser Expedition named this mountain in honour of Professor John H. Balfour, M.D. (1808–84). Dr. Balfour was a professor of botany at Glasgow University and the founder of the Botanical Society of Edinburgh. Mount Balfour is about 75 km northwest of Banff.

MOUNT BALINHARD (3130 m) This mountain took its name from one of the titles of the Earl of Southesk, Baron Balinhard. He came to Canada in 1859 and explored western Canada. The Ninth Earl of Southesk recounted his travels in his book *Saskatchewan and the Rocky Mountains.* Mount Balinhard is 54 km southeast of Jasper. (see Mount Southesk)

MOUNT BALL (3311 m) In 1858 Sir James Hector named this mountain near Banff after John Ball, Undersecretary of State for the Colonies. Ball had secured the required funding for the Palliser Expedition, which lasted from 1857 to 1860. The expedition, headed by John Palliser, undertook a comprehensive survey and exploration of the area between the 49th Parallel and the North Saskatchewan River from the Red River to the Rocky Mountains.

M

MOUNT BARLOW (3120 m) This mountain was named after Dr. Alfred E. Barlow (1861–1914), a member of the Geological Survey of Canada. Mount Barlow is 95 km northwest of Banff.

MOUNT BARRA (2515 m) It is believed this mountain may be named after one of the islands of the Outer Hebrides, near Scotland. Mount Barra is 86 km northwest of Jasper.

MOUNT BARWELL (1829 m) This mountain was named after C.S.W. Barwell of the Dominion Land Survey. Mount Barwell is 40 km southwest of Calgary.

MOUNT BAUERMAN (2377 m) This mountain near Waterton Park took its name from Hilary Bauerman. From 1858 to 1862, he was the geologist for the British Boundary Commission, which surveyed the border between British North America and the U.S. through present-day BC.

Bauerman later became a professor of geology, teaching in Sheffield and Woolwich, England.

MOUNT BAZALGETTE (2438 m) The name of this mountain honours the only Albertan to receive the Victoria Cross, the British Empire's highest military medal, in World War II. Ian Willoughby Bazalgette (1918–44), of Calgary, was a master bomber in the Royal Air Force and died courageously in the line of duty. Mount Bazalgette is located about 55 km west-northwest of Hinton.

MORE ABOUT IAN BAZALGETTE... *During a World War II bombing raid in France, the Lancaster bomber flown by Squadron Leader Ian Willoughby Bazalgette came under heavy anti-aircraft fire. Despite heavy damage to his bomber, Bazalgette successfully bombed the enemy target. He then ordered his crew to bail out, and Bazalgette single-handedly landed his burning aircraft, avoiding a crash in a nearby French village. Before he was able to escape from the plane, it exploded, and he lost his life. He was awarded the Victoria Cross for his courageous act and in 1973 was named to Canada's Aviation Hall of Fame.*

MOUNT BEATTY (2999 m) This mountain located about 70 km west of Turner Valley was named in honour of Vice-Admiral David Beatty (1871–1936) who commanded the British Grand Fleet during the 1916 Battle of Jutland.

MOUNT BEAUPRE (2778 m) A.O. Wheeler named this mountain about 40 km west-northwest of Jasper in 1923 after a guide who assisted Sir Sandford Fleming's Canadian Pacific Survey. The Canadian Pacific Survey, conducted from 1871 to 1876, sought a route for the transcontinental CPR line through the Rockies.

MOUNT BELANGER (3120 m) Dr. Donald Bogart Dowling (see Mount Bogart) named this mountain in 1921 after

André Belanger, who was with the party that crossed the Athabasca Pass in 1814. The same year he crossed the pass, Belanger drowned in the Athabasca River near Brûlé Lake. Mount Belanger is 43 km south of Jasper. (see Mount Lapensée)

MOUNT BELL (2190 m) This mountain took its name from Nora Bell, a member of the group that made the first ascent of the mountain. Mount Bell is about 40 km northwest of Banff.

MOUNT BERGNE (3176 m) A.O. Wheeler named this mountain in 1920 after Frank Bergne, a member of the Alpine Club of London. Bergne had died 13 years earlier while climbing with Wheeler in Switzerland. Mount Bergne is 110 km northwest of Banff.

MOUNT BESS (3216 m) This mountain was named in 1911 after Miss Bessie Gunn of Lac Ste. Anne. She later married M.C. McKeen, who served in the United Farmers of Alberta provincial government. Mount Bess is 103 km northwest of Jasper.

MOUNT BIRDWOOD (3097 m) This mountain was named after Field Marshal Sir William R. Birdwood (1865–1951). He commanded the Australian and New Zealand Army Corps during the Gallipoli campaign of World War I.

MOUNT BISHOP (2850 m) This mountain was named in honour of Air Marshal W.A. "Billy" Bishop (1894–1956). The Canadian air ace shot down 72 planes during World War I. He was awarded the British Empire's highest military medal, the Victoria Cross, as well as the Distinguished Service Order and the Military Cross. Mount Bishop is 48 km southwest of Turner Valley.

MOUNT BISTRE (2346 m) This is a descriptive name referring to the mountain's brown colour. Mount Bistre is about 38 km northwest of Jasper.

MOUNT BLACK PRINCE (2932 m) This mountain was named after a British cruiser that was destroyed in 1916 during the 1916 Battle of Jutland. The cruiser sank in the battle, and 750 of her crew died with her. Mount Black Prince is 70 km west of Turner Valley.

MOUNT BLAKISTON (2910 m) This mountain was named after Lieutenant Thomas Blakiston (1832–91) of the Royal Artillery. He was a magnetic observer on the Palliser Expedition from 1857 to 1860. In addition to recording magnetic observations, Blakiston, who had a strong interest in ornithology, noted many Alberta bird species. Mount Blakiston is near Waterton Lakes National Park.

MOUNT BLANE (2993 m) This mountain was named after Sir C.R. Blane, a commander of the battleship *Queen Mary*. The ship sank during the 1916 Battle of Jutland. Mount Blane is 55 km west of Turner Valley.

MOUNT BOGART (3144 m) This mountain about 75 km west of Calgary was named after Dr. Donald Bogart Dowling (1858–1925). Dr. Dowling was an early worker in the development of coal, petroleum and natural gas.

MOUNT BOLTON (2706 m) This mountain was named after L.E.S. Bolton of the Surveyor General's staff in Ottawa. He was killed in action in World War I. Mount Bolton is 52 km southwest of Turner Valley.

MOUNT BOSWELL (2400 m) This mountain was named after a veterinary surgeon with a British boundary commission. Mount Boswell is 55 km south of Pincher Creek.

MOUNT BOSWORTH (2771 m) This mountain was named after G.M. Bosworth, an executive of the Canadian Pacific Railway. Mount Bosworth is about 65 km northwest of Banff.

MOUNT BOURGEAU (2930 m) This mountain was named after Eugène Bourgeau, the botanist on the Palliser Expedition. Mount Bourgeau is near Banff.

MOUNT BOWLEN (3072 m) This mountain was named in honour of Dr. John James Bowlen (1876–1959). Dr. Bowlen sat as a Liberal member of the Alberta Legislature from 1931 to 1944 and served as Alberta's lieutenant-governor from 1950 to 1959. Mount Bowlen is 50 km northwest of Banff.

MOUNT BRAITHWAITE (2134 m) This mountain was named in honour of Edward A. Braithwaite, M.D. (1862–1949). He was a medical officer for the North-West Mounted Police and, in 1896, was named a coroner for the NWT. Mount Braithwaite is near Grande Cache.

MOUNT BRAZEAU (3470 m) This mountain 87 km west of Nordegg took its name from the Brazeau Range.

MOUNT BRETT (2984 m) This mountain was named after Robert George Brett, M.D. Dr. Brett was a surgeon with the CPR and served as Alberta's lieutenant-governor from 1915 to 1925. Mount Brett is near Banff.

MOUNT BREWSTER (2859 m) This mountain was named in honour of John Brewster. He was pioneer dairyman and father of the well-known Brewster family of the Banff area. Mount Brewster is near Banff.

MOUNT BRIDGLAND (2930 m) This mountain was named after Morrison Parsons Bridgland (1878–1948). He was a surveyor for the Dominion Lands Survey and a founding member of the Alpine Club of Canada. Mount Bridgland is 32 km northwest of Jasper.

MOUNT BROCK (2902 m) This mountain was named in honour of Rear Admiral Osmond de Beauvoir Brock.

M

Admiral Brock was engaged in the World War I Battle of Jutland. Mount Brock is 55 km northwest of Turner Valley.

MOUNT BROWN (2799 m) This mountain was named after Robert Brown, a Scottish botanist. Mount Brown is 57 km southwest of Jasper.

MOUNT BRYANT (2621 m) This mountain was named in honour of Frank Bryant. He held a number of senior positions in the Canadian Parks Department—warden of Jasper Park, chief warden at Waterton Lakes National Park and superintendent of Kootenay National Park. Mount Bryant is 60 km west of Calgary.

MOUNT BRYCE (3507 m) This mountain was named after Viscount James Bryce. Viscount Bryce was a president of the Alpine Club of London and at one time served as the British ambassador to the U.S. The mountain is 92 km southwest of Jasper.

MOUNT BULLER (2805 m) This mountain 80 km west of Calgary was named after Lieutenant Colonel H.C. Buller of the Princess Patricia's Canadian Light Infantry, who died during World War I.

MOUNT BULYEA (3304 m) This mountain was named after Alberta's first lieutenant-governor, George Hedly V. Bulyea. Mount Bulyea is 115 km northwest of Banff.

MOUNT BURKE (2542 m) This mountain 45 km southwest of Turner Valley was named after Denis Charles Burke. He was a rancher and forest ranger.

MOUNT BURNEY (2943 m) This mountain was named after Vice-Admiral Sir Cecil Burney, commander of the ship HMS *Marlborough* in the 1916 Battle of Jutland. Mount Burney is 55 km west of Turner Valley.

MOUNT BURNS (2936 m) This mountain about 41 km west of Turner Valley was named after Patrick Burns.

MORE ABOUT PATRICK BURNS...*Patrick Burns (1856–1937) had a humble start in life, but he became one of Canada's most successful businessmen. Born in Ontario, one of 10 children of Irish immigrants, Burns started in the meat-packing business almost by chance. When an employer in Ontario could not pay $100 cash for work Burns had done, Burns accepted a pair of oxen in payment. The oxen on the hoof were worth only $70, but by slaughtering them and selling the cuts of meat, Burns put $140 in his pocket. This was incentive for Burns to go to Calgary, where he started a small slaughterhouse. Riding on the railway construction boom, his business flourished, and he set up meat-packing plants across Canada, the U.S. and Britain. By the time of World War I, P. Burns and Co. Ltd. was a large international business. He sold his portion of the business for $15 million dollars in 1928. Burns also had vast cattle ranches that earned him the unofficial title of "Cattle King of the West." Burns was one of the "Big Four" who put up the money to start the Calgary Stampede. At age 75, Burns was appointed to the Canadian Senate.*

M

MOUNT BURSTALL (2760 m) This mountain took the name of Lieutenant General Sir E.H. Burstall, who commanded Canadian troops in World War I. Mount Burstall is 90 km southwest of Calgary, in the Spray Mountains range.

MOUNT BYNG (2940 m) This mountain was named after General Julian, First Viscount Byng of Vimy (1862–1935). He commanded the Canadian Army Corps from May 1916 to 1917. Viscount Byng served as governor general from 1921 to 1926. Mount Byng is about 100 km southwest of Calgary.

MOUNT CAMBRAI (3134 m) This mountain was named after a town of the same name in France. In October 1918, during the final offensive of World War I, Canadian troops captured Cambrai. Mount Cambrai is located about 120 km northwest of Banff.

MOUNT CAMPION (2484 m) This mountain was named to honour Corporal George Campion of Edmonton. He was killed in action in World War II. Mount Campion is 83 km northwest of Jasper.

MOUNT CARDINAL (2515 m) This mountain about 52 km east of Jasper was named after Jacques Cardinal, a local fur trader in the early 1900s.

MOUNT CARTHEW (2621 m) This mountain near Waterton Park was named after William M. Carthew, a survey assistant with Dominion Lands Survey.

MOUNT CAUTLEY (2880 m) This mountain was named after Richard W. Cautley of the Dominion Lands Survey. Cautley was a surveyor and the commissioner representing Alberta on the Alberta–BC Inter-Provincial Boundary Commission, which established the boundary between these two provinces. Mount Cautley is about 100 km west of Calgary.

MOUNT CHARLES STEWART (2809 m) This mountain near Canmore was named after Charles Stewart (1868–1946). Stewart was the Liberal premier of Alberta from 1917 to 1921. After being elected to the House of Commons, he held various federal Cabinet positions. Later he was appointed chairman of the International Joint Commission. Mount Charles Stewart is the highest peak in the Fairholme Range.

MOUNT CHARLTON (3217 m) This mountain 44 km southeast of Jasper was named after H.R. Charlton of the Grand Trunk Pacific Railway.

MOUNT CHEPHREN (3266 m) This mountain was named after Khafre, whose Greek name was Chephren. He was the fourth pharaoh of Ancient Egypt's Fourth Dynasty, who was thought to have ruled from about 2520 BC to about 2494 BC. The mountain was first called Pyramid Mountain, because it is shaped roughly like a pyramid. However, the name had to be changed to avoid confusion with Pyramid Mountain near Jasper. The name Chephren was chosen as a substitute because that pharaoh was behind the construction of one of the three Pyramids of Giza. Mount Chephren is 105 km northwest of Banff.

MOUNT CHESTER (3054 m) This mountain took its name from the cruiser HMS *Chester*. The ship was engaged in the World War I Battle of Jutland. Mount Chester is located 80 km west-southwest of Calgary.

MOUNT CHOWN (3381 m) This mountain 107 km northwest of Jasper was named after Reverend Samuel Dwight Chown, D.D., LL.D. Rev. Chown was General Superintendent of the Methodist Church and was influential in the formation of the United Church of Canada in 1925.

MOUNT CHRISTIE (3103 m) This mountain was named after William J. Christie, who held various positions with the Hudson's Bay Company. Mount Christie is 43 km southeast of Jasper.

MOUNT CLAIRVAUX (2690 m) *Clairvaux* is the French word for "clear valleys." The description suits this mountain, which is located at the head of a clear valley. Mount Clairvaux is 24 km southwest of Jasper.

MOUNT CLINE (3361 m) This mountain about 130 km southeast of Jasper was named after Michael Cline. He was an employee of the North West Company and the Hudson's Bay Company.

MOUNT CLITHEROE (2747 m) This mountain was named after a borough of Lancashire, England. Mount Clitheroe is near Jasper.

MOUNT COLEMAN (3135 m) This mountain 115 km southeast of Jasper was named after Arthur P. Coleman. He was an early alpinist in the Rockies.

MOUNT COLIN (2687 m) This mountain was named after Colin Fraser (ca. 1805–67). He was employed with the Hudson's Bay Company and ran Jasper House from 1835 to 1849. Fraser also served as Sir George Simpson's private piper. Mount Colin is approximately 115 km southeast of Jasper.

MOUNT COLUMBIA (3747 m) Mount Columbia and the Columbia Icefield were named for the Columbia River, which was itself named after the ship of U.S. sea captain Robert Tray. In 1792, Tray successfully crossed the dangerous bar at the river's mouth in his ship *Columbia Rediviva*. Mount Columbia is the highest point in Alberta and is located about 90 km southeast of Jasper.

MOUNT CONFEDERATION (2969 m) This mountain about 60 km southeast of Jasper was named in honour of Canada's Fathers of Confederation.

MOUNT CONWAY (3100 m) This mountain was named after William M. Conway, famed mountaineer and art historian. Mount Conway is about 105 km northwest of Banff.

MOUNT CORDONNIER (3021 m) This mountain was named in honour of French general Victor Louis E. Cordonnier. He distinguished himself in World War I and World War II. Mount Cordonnier is about 70 km west-southwest of Turner Valley.

MOUNT CORNWELL (2972 m) This mountain approximately 46 km west of Turner Valley was named in 1918 after John Travers Cornwell, V.C. He was a boy hero during the Battle of Jutland. Cornwell was assigned the duty of relaying orders from the gunnery to the crew. He was wounded during action but stayed at his post. Cornwell died after the battle from his wounds and was posthumously awarded the Victoria Cross, the British Empire's highest military medal, for bravery.

MOUNT CORY (2802 m) This mountain near Banff was named after William W. Cory, deputy minister of the Interior in Ottawa from 1905 to 1930.

MOUNT COSTIGAN (2980 m) This mountain near Canmore was named after John Costigan. He held many cabinet positions in the late 1800s and was appointed to the Senate in 1907.

MOUNT CÔTÉ (2391 m) This mountain was named after Senator Jean Léon Côté (1867–1924). He was a member of the Alberta Legislature before being appointed to the Senate in 1923. Mount Côté is 48 km west of Grande Cache. (see Jean Côté)

M

MOUNT COULTHARD (2642 m) This mountain near Coleman was named after R.W. Coulthard, a mining engineer and manager of the Western Canadian Coal Company in the early 1900s.

MOUNT CRANDELL (2381 m) This mountain about 45 km south of Pincher Creek was named after Edward H. Crandell (1859–1944). He was a Calgary businessman, city councillor and schoolboard trustee.

MOUNT CROMWELL (3330 m) This mountain was named after Oliver Eaton Cromwell. He was a member of the French, British and American alpine clubs and, in 1936, was in the first party to climb this mountain. Mount Cromwell is about 80 km southeast of Jasper.

MOUNT CUMNOCK (2460 m) This mountain took its name from Cumnock, Ayrshire, Scotland. Mount Cumnock is about 34 km north-northwest of Jasper.

MOUNT CURRIE (2810 m) This mountain was named in honour of Sir Arthur W. Currie, K.C.B., K.C.M.G. Sir Arthur (1875–1933) commanded the Canadian army in 1917 and later was vice-chancellor of McGill University.

MOUNT DALHOUSIE (2438 m) This mountain approximately 61 km west-northwest of Nordegg was named after the 11th Earl of Dalhousie (1801–74), the British Secretary for War during the Crimean War.

MOUNT DALY (3152 m) This mountain was named after Chief Justice Charles P. Daly, president of the American Geographical Society. Mount Daly is about 70 km northwest of Banff.

MOUNT DARRAH (2755 m) This mountain, located near Coleman, was named after Captain Charles J. Darrah, an astronomer with the 1858–62 British Boundary Commission. Mount Darrah was previously known as Gable Mountain.

MOUNT DAVID (2780 m) This mountain was named after David Thompson (1770–1857). This explorer compiled some of the first maps of western Canada. Mount David is 115 km northwest of Banff.

MOUNT De VEBER (2573 m) This mountain about 40 km southwest of Grande Cache was named in honour of Leverett George de Veber, M.D. Dr. de Veber (1848–1925) was a physician and surgeon with the Royal North-West Mounted Police and was elected to the Alberta Legislature in 1905. Shortly after his election, Dr. de Veber was appointed to the Senate and served there until 1925.

MOUNT De WIND (2438 m) This mountain approximately 81 km northwest of Jasper was named after Second Lieutenant Edmund De Wind, V.C. He was awarded the Victoria Cross, the British Empire's highest military medal, for bravery in World War I.

MOUNT DENT (3267 m) This mountain was named after Clinton T. Dent, M.A., M.C., F.R.C.S. He was a surgeon, avid mountaineer and president of the Alpine Club of London, England, in the late 1800s.

MOUNT DOUGLAS (3235 m) This mountain was named after David Douglas. He was a Scottish botanist who crossed the Rocky Mountains via Athabasca Pass in 1827. After being appointed botanical collector for the Horticultural Society in London, Douglas travelled to the United States and Canada, collecting seeds and specimens of a variety of plants. The Douglas fir was named after him. Mount Douglas is about 50 km northwest of Banff. (see Mount St. Bride)

MOUNT DRINNAN (2242 m) This mountain near Hinton was named after R.G. Drinnan, manager of Cadomin Mine and later director of Luscar Collieries.

MOUNT DROMORE (2621 m) This mountain near Jasper was named after a town in County Down, Ireland. *Dromore* is Celtic for "great ridge."

MOUNT DRUMMOND (3148 m) This mountain about 60 km northwest of Banff was named after Thomas Drummond. He was the assistant naturalist on Sir Franklin's Second Arctic Expedition of 1825–27.

MOUNT DYSON (1768 m) This mountain was named after a local rancher. Mount Dyson is near Turner Valley.

MOUNT EDITH (2554 m) This mountain was named after Mrs. Edith Orde (née Cox). Edith visited Banff with Lady Macdonald, wife of Prime Minister Sir John A. Macdonald, in 1886. Mount Edith is near Banff.

MOUNT EDITH CAVELL (3363 m) Mount Edith Cavell is located about 24 km south of Jasper. This mountain was named after World War I nurse Edith Cavell.

M

MORE ABOUT EDITH CAVELL...*Edith Cavell (1865–1915) was a nurse during World War I, serving as a matron in a Red Cross hospital in Brussells where many wounded soldiers were sent. She aided British and French troops trapped behind the German lines and helped them rejoin their armies. For this, the Germans executed her. Cavell did not deny her activity when captured by the Germans. Her legal defence was based on her duty as a nurse to save lives. She was killed by a German firing squad. This was within the rules of war, but her execution proved to be a blunder for the Germans. Within days, Cavell was seen as a martyr, and Allied morale was strengthened. Six months after her death, this mountain was named in her memory. After the war, Cavell's body was brought in state to Westminster Abbey and buried in Norwich Cathedral. Numerous books have been written, and films produced, honouring her life.*

M

MOUNT ENGELHARD (3270 m) This mountain was named after Georgia Engelhard. She was an avid mountaineer and also the author of the children's book *Peterli and the Mountain*. Mount Engelhard is located 80 km southeast of Jasper.

MOUNT ERASMUS (3265 m) This mountain was named after Peter Erasmus (1834–1931). This pioneer, trader and noted guide accompanied the Palliser Expedition. Mount Erasmus is about 125 km northwest of Banff.

MOUNT ERRIS (2820 m) This mountain about 30 km northwest of Coleman was named after a headland in County Mayo, Ireland.

MOUNT EVANS (3210 m) This mountain was named after Captain E.R.G. Evans. He was second in command of the British 1910–12 Antarctic Expedition and after the death of Captain Scott became the expedition's leader. Mount Evans is about 49 km south of Jasper.

MOUNT EVAN-THOMAS (3097 m) This mountain about 70 km west-southwest of Calgary was named after Rear Admiral H. Evan-Thomas. He took part in the 1916 Battle of Jutland.

MOUNT FARQUHAR (2905 m) This mountain about 60 km southwest of Turner Valley was named after Lieutenant Colonel F.D. Farquhar. He commanded the Princess Patricia's Canadian Light Infantry and was killed in World War I.

MOUNT FAY (3235 m) This mountain about 45 km west-northwest of Banff was named after Professor Charles E. Fay. An avid mountaineer, he founded the Appalachian Mountain Club and the American Alpine Club.

MOUNT FOCH (3180 m) This mountain was named after Marshal Ferdinand Foch, who commanded the Allied forces in 1918.

MOUNT FORBES (3612 m) This mountain was named after British naturalist Professor Edward Forbes. Mount Forbes is about 120 km northwest of Banff.

MOUNT FORGET (2121 m) This mountain was named after Amedée Emmanuel Forget (1847–1923). He served as lieutenant-governor of the North-West Territories from 1898 to 1905 and later was named to the Senate.

MOUNT FORTUNE (2819 m) This mountain was named after a destroyer that took part in the 1916 Battle of Jutland. Mount Fortune is 80 km west-southwest of Calgary.

MOUNT FRASER (3269 m) This mountain was named after Simon Fraser (1776–1862). This fur trader and explorer discovered the Fraser River. Mount Fraser is near Jasper.

MOUNT FRENCH (3234 m) This mountain was named after Field Marshal John Denton P. French, commander-in-chief of the British army from 1914 to 1915. In 1922, he was named Viscount of Ypres. Mount French is about 70 km northwest of Turner Valley.

MOUNT FRESHFIELD (3336 m) This mountain 115 km northwest of Banff was named after Douglas W. Freshfield. He was a mountaineer and member of the Alpine Club.

MOUNT FRYATT (3361 m) This mountain about 37 km south-southeast of Jasper was named after Captain Charles Algernon Fryatt (1872–1916). He was a merchant seaman World War I hero who was shot by the Germans for his attempt to ram their submarine with his ship. Brussels Peak and Fryatt Creek are also named in memory of this event.

MOUNT GALATEA (3185 m) This mountain about 80 km west of Calgary was named after a British cruiser that took part in the 1916 Battle of Jutland.

MOUNT GALWEY (2377 m) This mountain was named after Lieutenant Galwey. He was with the British complement of the North American Boundary Commission (1872–74). The Commission defined the Canada–U.S. border from the Lake of the Woods to the Rocky Mountains. Mount Galwey is about 40 km south of Pincher Creek.

MOUNT GARTH (3030 m) This mountain was named after the hometown of a well-known North West Company employee. John McDonald, of Garth, served with the North West Company in western Canada from 1791 to 1813. Mount Garth is about 115 km northwest of Banff.

MOUNT GASS (2865 m) This mountain about 70 km southwest of Turner Valley was named after L.H. Gass. He worked for the Dominion Lands Survey before being killed in World War I.

MOUNT GAUNCE (2286 m) This mountain 80 km northwest of Jasper was named after Squadron Leader Lionel M. Gaunce. During World War II, he earned the Distinguished Flying Cross and died in action.

MOUNT GEC (3130 m) The name for this mountain was taken from the initials of the Christian names of the first three climbers to scale this peak. They were George Harr, Ellen Wilts and Chuck Wilts. Mount Gec is about 74 km south-southeast of Jasper.

MOUNT GIROUARD (2995 m) This mountain near Banff was named after Colonel Sir Eduard Girouard, K.C.M.G., D.S.O. Born in Montréal, Girouard (1867–1932) served as a railway builder in North Africa and South Africa during the expansion of the British Empire in the late 1800s. Girouard served as Canada's director general of munitions supply in 1915.

MOUNT GLADSTONE (2370 m) This mountain was named after William S. Gladstone. Nicknamed "Old Glad," he was with the Hudson's Bay Company and later was one of the builders of Fort Whoop-up in southern Alberta. Mount Gladstone is southwest of Pincher Creek.

MOUNT GLASGOW (2935 m) This mountain about 60 km west-southwest of Calgary was named after a cruiser that took part in the 1916 Battle of Jutland.

MOUNT GLENDOWAN (2673 m) This mountain was named after the Glendowan Range in Ireland. Mount Glendowan is near Waterton Lakes National Park.

MOUNT GORMAN (2340 m) This mountain about 65 km northwest of Grande Cache was named after A.O. Gorman. He was with the Dominion Land Survey.

MOUNT GRIESBACH (2682 m) This mountain near Jasper was named after William A. Griesbach (1878–1945).

M

William Antrobus Griesbach received many decorations during his life of service: C.B., C.M.G., D.S.O., V.D. and the K.C. Called to the bar in 1901, this highly decorated and distinguished soldier-statesman was a Boer War veteran, an Edmonton alderman and mayor, and during World War I, a lieutenant colonel of the Canadian Expeditionary Force in France and a brigadier general of the First Canadian Infantry Brigade. He was elected to the House of Commons in 1917 and was later made a senator. Griesbach was promoted to major general in the Canadian Army in 1921 and was inspector general for the Western Canadian militia from 1940 to 1943.

MOUNT HABEL (3073 m) This mountain was named after Jean Habel. He explored the region in the late 1800s. Mount Habel is 90 km northwest of Banff.

MOUNT HAIG (2610 m) This mountain was named after Captain R.W. Haig. He was a senior official with the British Boundary Commission. Mount Haig is about 40 km southwest of Pincher Creek.

MOUNT HARDISTY (2700 m) This mountain located near Jasper was named after Senator Hardisty. (see Hardisty)

MOUNT HARRIS (3299 m) This mountain was named after L.E. Harris of the Dominion Land Survey who was the first person to climb it. Mount Harris is about 80 km northwest of Banff.

MOUNT HARVEY (2438 m) This mountain about 83 km north-northwest of Jasper was named after Lieutenant F. M.W. Harvey, V.C., M.C. Harvey, of Fort Macleod, was killed in World War I.

MOUNT HAULTAIN (2621 m) This mountain was named after Sir Fredrick William A.G. Haultain, K.C., LL.B. He practised law at Fort Macleod and was a member of the government of the North-West Territories from 1887 to 1905. Haultain played an important role in guiding Alberta and Saskatchewan to provincehood. He served as a MLA and a chief justice in Saskatchewan and as chancellor of the University of Saskatchewan. Mount Haultain is about 37 km north-northwest of Jasper.

MOUNT HAWKINS (2682 m) This mountain just northwest of Waterton Lakes National Park was named after Lieutenant Colonel John Summerfields Hawkins, commissioner of the 1858–62 British Boundary Commission.

MOUNT HEAD (2782 m) This mountain 36 km southwest of Turner Valley was named after Sir Edmund Walker Head (1805–68). He was governor general of British North America from 1854 to 1861 and later was governor of the Hudson's Bay Company.

MOUNT HECTOR (3394 m) This mountain was named after Sir James Hector, M.D., C.M.G., K.C.M.G. He was the surgeon, geologist and second-in-command of the Palliser Expedition. The Palliser Expedition was charged with surveying between the 49th Parallel and the North Saskatchewan River from the Red River to the Rocky Mountains. The expedition also tried to determine the viability of a railway line south of the Athabasca Pass. Mount Hector is about 65 km northwest of Banff. (For more on Sir James Hector, see Kicking Horse Pass)

M

MOUNT HENDAY (2682 m) This mountain near Jasper was named after Anthony Henday. He was a fur trader and the first European to set foot in now what is Alberta, arriving in the vicinity of present-day Chauvin in 1754. He was the first European known to have seen the Rockies.

MOUNT HENRY MacLEOD (3288 m) This mountain took its name from Henry A.F. MacLeod, an engineer with the Canadian Pacific Railway. Mount Henry MacLeod is about 85 km west of Nordegg.

MOUNT HOFFMAN (1829 m) This mountain about 28 km west of Turner Valley was named after one Mr. Hoffman. He was a member of a survey party.

MOUNT HOOD (2903 m) This mountain was named after Horace Hood. He was a rear admiral in the British Navy and died in the sinking of the HMS *Invincible* (see Mount Invincible) during the 1916 Battle of Jutland. Mount Hood is about 55 km west-northwest of Turner Valley.

MOUNT HOOGE (3216 m) This mountain 120 km south-east of Jasper was named for a village near Ypres, Belgium where Canadian troops fought during World War I.

M

MOUNT HOOKER (3286 m) This mountain was named after Sir William Jackson Hooker, an English botanist and a director of Kew Gardens, England. Mount Hooker is about 53 km south of Jasper.

MOUNT HOWARD (2777 m) This mountain about 60 km west of Calgary was named after Terrence Howard, a homesteader and forest ranger in the area.

MOUNT HUESTIS (3063 m) This mountain 85 km northwest of Banff was named in honour of Eric S. Huestis, Alberta's deputy minister of Lands and Forest. Huestis made a contribution to the management of the province's forests.

MOUNT INFLEXIBLE (3000 m) This mountain about 80 km west-southwest of Calgary was named after a British naval vessel engaged in the 1916 Battle of Jutland.

MOUNT INGLISMALDIE (2964 m) This mountain near Banff was named in the 1880s after Inglismaldie Castle, Scotland. The castle was the seat of the Earl of Kintore, who was visiting Banff when the mountain was named.

MOUNT INVINCIBLE (2670 m) This mountain was named after the HMS *Invincible*. This cruiser sank during the 1916 Battle of Jutland. Only six of the ship's crew of 1034 survived. Rear-Admiral Horace Hood (see Mount Hood) died in the sinking. Mount Invincible is about 64 km west of Turner Valley.

MOUNT ISAAC (2632 m) This mountain about 61 km west of Nordegg was named after local trapper Isaac Plante.

MOUNT ISHBEL (2908 m) This mountain was named after Ishbel MacDonald. She was the daughter of British Prime Minister Ramsay MacDonald. Mount Ishbel is about 35 km west-southwest of Banff.

MOUNT JAMES WALKER (3035 m) This mountain was named after Colonel James Walker. He was with the North-West Mounted Police and later became a businessman. Mount James Walker is about 80 km west-southwest of Calgary.

MOUNT JELLICOE (3246 m) This mountain was named after Sir John R. Jellicoe. He commanded the British Grand Fleet during the 1916 Battle of Jutland. Mount Jellicoe is located about 70 km west of Turner Valley.

MOUNT JERRAM (2996 m) This mountain 55 km west of Turner Valley was named after Admiral Sir Thomas Jerram, leader of the Second Battle Squadron during the 1916 Battle of Jutland.

M

MOUNT JESSIE (2652 m) This mountain 95 km northwest of Jasper was named after Jessie Campbell. She was the sister of A.J. Campbell of the Dominion Lands Survey.

MOUNT JOFFRE (3450 m) This mountain about 70 km west-southwest of Turner Valley was named after Marshal J.J. Joffre. He was commander-in-chief of the French Army from 1915 to 1917.

MOUNT KANE (3090 m) This mountain was named after the famous Canadian artist-explorer, Paul Kane. He travelled from Toronto to the Pacific Coast from 1845 to 1848 and recorded his impressions in *Wandering of an Artist Among the Indians of North America.* Mount Kane is 49 km south of Jasper.

MOUNT KENTIGERN (3176 m) This mountain was named after St. Kentigern. He lived in the sixth century and was bishop of Strathclyde in Scotland. Mount Kentigern is about 85 km northwest of Banff.

M

MOUNT KERR (2560 m) This mountain was named after Private John C. Kerr, V.C. During World War I, this resident of Edmonton was in the Canadian Expeditionary Force's 49th Battalion and was awarded the Victoria Cross, the British Empire's highest military medal, for his bravery under fire. He died during the war. Mount Kerr is near Jasper.

MOUNT KIDD (2928 m) This mountain 75 km west of Calgary was named after Stuart Kidd, a pioneer and businessman who was fluent in Stoney. He was later made honorary chief of the Stoney.

MOUNT KING ALBERT (2987 m) This mountain west of Turner Valley was named after King Albert of Belgium. He was popular with his people and was regarded as a World War I hero. Albert died while mountain climbing in 1934.

MOUNT KING EDWARD (3490 m) This mountain was named in honour of King Edward VII who became king in 1901.

MOUNT KINROSS (2560 m) This mountain near Jasper was named after Private Cecil John Kinross, V.C. During World War I, Kinross, of Calgary, joined the Canadian Army's 49th Battalion and won a Victoria Cross for charging an enemy machine gun position and killing several of its soldiers.

MOUNT KITCHENER (3505 m) This mountain was named after Horatio H. Kitchener. During World War I, Viscount Kitchener was Britain's field marshal and secretary of state for war from 1914 to 1916. Mount Kitchener is about 90 km southeast of Jasper.

MOUNT KNIGHT (2845 m) This mountain was named after Richard M. Knight. He was a superintendent at Jasper National Park. Mount Knight is about 35 km northwest of Jasper.

M

MOUNT LA GRACE (2822 m) This mountain 60 km east of Jasper was named after a Métis hunter who journeyed with Lord Southesk to the Rocky Mountains in 1859.

MOUNT LAMBE (3182 m) This mountain was named after Lawrence M. Lambe. He was a palaeontologist with the Geological Survey of Canada. Mount Lambe is 110 km northwest of Banff.

MOUNT LAPENSÉE (3106 m) This mountain was named after Oliver R. Lapensée. Lapensée, with Gabriel Franchère (of Franchère Peak fame) and André Belanger (of Mount Belanger fame), crossed the Athabasca Pass in 1814. The same year they crossed the pass, Lapensée and Belanger drowned in the Athabasca River near Brûlé Lake. Mount Lapensée is about 40 km south of Jasper.

MOUNT LAURIE (2195 m) This mountain near Canmore was named after Dr. John Laurie (1895–1959). He was an advocate of Aboriginal rights and founded the Indian Association of Alberta. He was made honorary chief of the Stoney, Sarcee and Blood. The University of Alberta awarded Laurie an honorary doctorate. Dr. Laurie wrote a Stoney dictionary.

MOUNT LAUT (2408 m) This mountain was named after Wing Commander A. Laut, M.I.D. During World War II, he served with a Coastal Command squadron in Canada and died in a flying accident. Mount Laut is about 80 km north-northwest of Jasper.

MOUNT LAWSON (2795 m) This mountain 75 km west-southwest of Calgary was named after Major W.E. Lawson of the Geological Survey.

MOUNT LEFROY (3423 m) In 1858 this mountain was named by Sir James Hector of the Palliser Expedition after General Sir John H. Lefroy, R.A. Lefroy was a noted astronomer. During the winter of 1843, he recorded magnetic observations at Fort Chipewyan, Fort Dunvegan (today's Dunvegan) and Fort Edmonton (today's Edmonton), as well as several places in today's NWT. He was head of the Toronto Observatory from 1842 to 1853. Mount Lefroy is about 55 km west-northwest of Banff.

MOUNT LEMAN (2730 m) This mountain was named after General G. Leman. He led the defence of Liege, Belgium in World War I. Mount Leman is about 80 km west-northwest of Turner Valley.

MOUNT LEVAL (2713 m) This mountain was named after Gaston de Leval. He was the Belgian lawyer who defended Edith Cavell (of Mount Edith Cavell fame) in court. Mount Leval is located about 85 km west-southwest of Calgary.

MOUNT LINDSAY (2743 m) The Earl of Southesk named this mountain after his friend Sir Coutts Lindsay. Lindsay's home in Scotland is commemorated in the name of nearby Mount Balcarres. Mount Lindsay is about 47 km east of Jasper.

MOUNT LIPSETT (2560 m) This mountain was named after Major General L.J. Lipsett. He was with the Canadian Expeditionary Force during World War I. Mount Lipsett is about 55 km west-southwest of Turner Valley.

MOUNT LITTLE (3088 m) This mountain took its name from George F. Little. He was one of the original group to climb this mountain. Mount Little is located 52 km west-northwest of Banff.

MOUNT LIVINGSTONE (3090 m) This mountain 60 km west-northwest of Claresholm was named after Dr. David Livingstone. He was a doctor, missionary, African explorer and one of the first to call for the abolition of the slave trade. (see Livingstone Range)

M

MOUNT LORETTE (2469 m) This mountain was named following World War I after the Lorett Ridge in France. Mount Lorette is about 70 km west of Calgary.

MOUNT LOUGHEED (3105 m) This mountain about 80 km west of Calgary was named after Sir James Alexander Lougheed. (see Lougheed)

MOUNT LOUIE (1844 m) It is thought this mountain may have been named after Native oldtimer Louie Delorme. Mount Louie is near Grande Cache.

MOUNT LOW (2722 m) This mountain was named after A.P. Low, an Arctic explorer and head of the Dominion Land Survey in the early 1900s. Mount Low is about 90 km northwest of Banff.

MOUNT LYALL (2950 m) This mountain was named after Dr. David Lyall, M.D. He was a surgeon and naturalist for the 1858–62 British Boundary Commission. Mount Lyall is about 70 km southwest of Turner Valley.

MOUNT LYAUTEY (3082 m) This mountain 70 km west-southwest of Turner Valley was named after General L. H.G. Lyautey. He was a member of the French Academy and France's war minister in 1916.

MOUNT LYELL (3504 m) This mountain about 140 km northwest of Banff was named after a British geologist who was part of the British Survey Commission. Sir Charles Lyell worked in Europe and North America.

MOUNT MACCARIB (2749 m) This mountain took its name from the Quinnipiac Native word for "caribou." Caribou were in the area at the time the mountain was named. Mount Maccarib is 21 km southwest of Jasper.

M

MOUNT MACHRAY (2749 m) This mountain was named after the Most Reverend Robert Machray. He was an Anglican bishop of Rupert's Land, then became archbishop of Rupert's Land, and finally was primate of Canada. In the late 1800s he was named chancellor of the University of Manitoba. Mount Machray is about 50 km west-northwest of Jasper. (Strange but true: This mountain and the previous listing Mount Maccarib are the same height.)

MOUNT MACKENZIE (2764 m) Mount Mackenzie, 56 km east of Jasper, was named after D.M. Mackenzie. He was a forest supervisor on the Brazeau Reserve.

MOUNT MACLAREN (2286 m) This mountain was named after Brigadier General Charles H. Maclaren. He commanded a brigade of Canadian artillery during World War I. Mount Maclaren is about 49 km southwest of Turner Valley.

MOUNT MAHOOD (2896 m) This mountain about 37 km west-northwest of Jasper was named after a Canadian Pacific Railway engineer.

MOUNT MALLOCH (3068 m) This mountain was named after George Malloch. In addition to being one of the first to climb this mountain, Malloch was a Canadian geologist who was responsible for mapping this area. Mount Malloch is about 80 km northwest of Banff.

MOUNT MANGIN (3057 m) This mountain about 70 km west-southwest of Turner Valley was named after French World War I hero General Charles E. Mangin. He held the Grand Cross of the Legion of Honour, served on the Supreme War Council and was in charge of the Supreme Council of National Defence.

MOUNT MARLBOROUGH (2973 m) This mountain was named after a battleship that took part in the 1916 Battle of Jutland. Mount Marlborough is about 65 km west-southwest of Turner Valley.

MOUNT MARY VAUX (3200 m) This mountain about 55 km south-southeast of Jasper was named after Mary Vaux. A member of the Alpine Club, she took a great interest in the Rocky Mountains. Vaux was also known for her work with charities.

MOUNT MATKIN (2418 m) This mountain about 28 km northwest of Waterton Park was named after Philip K. Matkin, RCAF. He died during World War II.

MOUNT MAUDE (3042 m) This mountain was named in honour of Major General Sir Frederick S. Maude (1864–1917). Maude, a British officer, served in the Sudan and in the Boer War before serving as military secretary to Governor General Earl of Minto from 1901 to 1904. In 1917, during World War I, he led the British troops who captured

Baghdad, an important centre in the Ottoman Empire. Mount Maude is 70 km west of Turner Valley.

MOUNT MCBETH (2845 m) This mountain took its name from Morrison McBeth. He was a member of Lord Southesk's exploration party in 1859. Mount McBeth is about 64 km east-southeast of Jasper.

MOUNT MCCONNELL (3109 m) This mountain 60 km northwest of Banff was named after Richard G. McConnell. He was with the Geological Survey of Canada in the late 1800s.

MOUNT MCDOUGALL (2591 m) This mountain west of Calgary was named after Reverend George McDougall and his sons David and John. Rev. McDougall worked for years with the Stoney Natives.

MOUNT MCGILLIVRAY (2454 m) This mountain was named after Duncan McGillivray. He was with the North West Company and set up a trading post at Rocky Mountain House in 1799. Mount McGillivray is near Canmore.

MOUNT MCGUIRE (3030 m) This mountain 70 km southeast of Jasper was named after Fenton John A. McGuire, chief warden of Jasper National Park.

MOUNT MCHARG (2888 m) This mountain was named after Lieutenant Colonel Hart McHarg. He was killed in action in World War I. Mount McHarg is near Jasper.

MOUNT MCKEAN (2743 m) This mountain northwest of Jasper took its name from Captain George B. McKean, V.C., M.C., M.M. McKean (1888–1926) served with the Canadian Expeditionary Force in World War I.

MOUNT MCLAREN (2286 m) This mountain near Coleman was named in honour of Ontario senator Peter McLaren.

He was one of Ontario's "lumber kings" who helped develop lumbering in the Crowsnest Pass.

MOUNT MCNAB (1690 m) This mountain near Turner Valley was named after an oldtimer in the area, Sandy McNab.

MOUNT MCPHAIL (2883 m) This mountain was named after N.R. McPhail. He was with the Surveyor General's staff and was killed in World War I. Mount McPhail is about 50 km southwest of Turner Valley.

MOUNT MCQUEEN (2286 m) This mountain near Grande Cache was named after Dr. David G. McQueen. He was minister of the First Presbyterian Church in Edmonton from 1887 to 1930.

MOUNT MERCER (2970 m) This mountain 95 km west of Calgary was named after Major General M.S. Mercer. He was killed in action in World War I.

MOUNT MERLIN (2711 m) This mountain near Jasper took its name from Merlin in Alfred Lord Tennyson's "Idylls of the Kings."

M

MOUNT MICHENER (2545 m) This mountain 120 km northwest of Banff was named after Roland Michener (1900–91). He was governor general from 1967 to 1974.

MOUNT MIST (3057 m) This descriptive name refers to the clouds that gather around the mountain, giving it a misty appearance. Mount Mist is about 46 km west of Turner Valley.

MOUNT MORDEN LONG (3040 m) This mountain was named after Professor Morden H. Long of the University of Alberta. He was chairman of the Geographic Board of Alberta. Mount Morden Long is about 60 km south-southeast of Jasper.

MOUNT MOREN (2562 m) This mountain was named after Arthur Moren, M.D. He was a member of Sandford Fleming's Canadian Pacific Survey, conducted from 1871 to 1876, which sought a route through the Rockies for the transcontinental CPR line. Mount Morden is about 34 km west-northwest of Jasper.

MOUNT MORRISON (2896 m) This mountain about 95 km southwest of Calgary was named after Major-General Sir Edward W.B. Morrison. He commanded the Canadian Corps Artillery during World War I and later served as editor-in-chief of the *Ottawa Citizen* newspaper.

MOUNT MUIR (2758 m) This mountain southwest of Turner Valley was named after Alexander Muir (1830–1906). He was the author of the 1867 patriotic song "Maple Leaf Forever."

MOUNT MURCHISON (3390 m) Sir James Hector, second in command of the Palliser Expedition, named this mountain after Sir Roderick Murchison, a Scottish geologist and director general of the Geological Survey of Great Britain. Murchison had recommended Hector to the Palliser Expedition. Mount Murchison is about 125 km northwest of Banff.

MOUNT MURRAY (3024 m) This mountain about 85 km west-southwest of Calgary was named after Sir A.J. Murray. He was chief of the British Imperial General Staff and commanded British forces in Egypt in the early 1900s.

MOUNT NIBLOCK (2976 m) This mountain 60 km northwest of Banff was named after Canadian Pacific Railway superintendent John Niblock. (see Claresholm)

MOUNT NIVERVILLE (2963 m) This mountain about 115 km northwest of Banff was named after Joseph Claude Boucher de Niverville, a soldier and explorer. De Niverville and a party of men travelled up the Saskatchewan River to build Fort de Jonquière, a fur-trading post, in 1751. The fort's location is unknown. It lasted only one year.

MOUNT NORQUAY (2522 m) This mountain near Banff was named after John Norquay, who climbed this mountain. Norquay served as premier of Manitoba from 1878 to 1887.

MOUNT NORTHOVER (3048 m) This mountain 70 km west-southwest of Turner Valley took its name from Lieutenant A.W. Northover, V.C., a member of the Canadian Expeditionary Force during World War I.

MOUNT NOYES (3060 m) This mountain was named after Rev. Charles L. Noyes. He was a member of the Appalachian Mountain Club and was the first to climb several different mountains in the Rockies. Mount Noyes is about 105 km northwest of Banff.

MOUNT O'HAGAN (2445 m) This mountain was named after Dr. Thomas O'Hagan. When he arrived in Jasper in 1924 he established the Seton Hospital. Mount O'Hagan is about 37 km south-southwest of Hinton.

M

MOUNT OATES (3120 m) This mountain 48 km south of Jasper was named after Captain Oates (1880–1912), a member of Captain Scott's 1910–12 British Antarctic Expedition.

MOUNT ODLUM (2670 m) This mountain 50 km southwest of Turner Valley was named after Brigadier General V.W. Odlum, a member of the World War I Canadian Expeditionary Force.

MOUNT OLIVE (3130 m) This mountain 80 km northwest of Banff was named after the wife of mountaineer H.B. Dixon.

MOUNT OLIVER (2865 m) This mountain near Jasper was named after Frank Oliver (1853–1933). He founded the *Edmonton Bulletin* and served as an MP and a federal cabinet minister. (There is another Mount Oliver near Banff. The origin of its name is unknown.)

MOUNT OUTRAM (3240 m) This mountain was named after Sir James Outram, Baronet. He made the first ascents of many of the highest mountains in Rockies. Outram was the author of *In the Heart of the Canadian Rockies*. Mount Outram is about 120 km northwest of Banff.

MOUNT PACKENHAM (3000 m) This mountain about 70 km west-southwest of Calgary was named after Rear Admiral W.C. Packenham, a British officer who participated in the 1916 Battle of Jutland.

MOUNT PALMER (3150 m) This mountain was named after Howard Palmer. He was a mountaineer of the Rockies and took extensive photographs of the region. Mount Palmer is about 68 km southeast of Jasper.

MOUNT PARRISH (2530 m) This mountain near Coleman was named after Sherman Parrish, a homesteader in the Crowsnest Pass.

M

MOUNT PATTERSON (3197 m) This mountain about 95 km northwest of Banff was named after John D. Patterson. He was an avid mountaineer and former president of the Alpine Club of Canada.

MOUNT PATTISON (2316 m) This mountain was named after Private George Pattison, V.C. He was killed in action in World War I and was awarded the Victoria Cross for bravery. Mount Pattison is near Jasper.

MOUNT PAUL (2805 m) This mountain was named after Paul Sharples in 1911. At the age of nine, he was the first white child to visit the Maligne Lake area when he accompanied Mary Schäffer on her 1911 expedition. Schäffer wrote an account of their expedition, which was later published in *A Hunter of Peace*. Mount Paul is about 53 km southeast of Jasper. (see Samson Peak)

MOUNT PAULINE (2653 m) This mountain 65 km south-west of Grande Cache was named after the agent general for British Columbia, F.A. Pauline.

MOUNT PEECHEE (2935 m) This mountain near Banff was named in 1884 by Dr. G.M. Dawson of the Geological Survey of Canada. He named it after Piché, a Métis guide to Sir George Simpson. In the everyday use of the name, "Piché" has become "Peechee."

MOUNT PENGELLY (2560 m) This mountain near Coleman took its name from the family name of A.J. Campbell's wife. Campbell was with the Alberta–British Columbia Boundary Commission.

MOUNT PERREN (3051 m) This mountain about 50 km west-northwest of Banff was named after Walter Perren. He was a Swiss mountain guide who came to Canada in 1950 and developed search-and-rescue techniques still in use today.

MOUNT PESKETT (3124 m) This mountain 105 km northwest of Banff was named after Louis Peskett. He was noted for his work with troubled teenagers and advanced the idea of setting up a camp for these teenagers. Peskett was a director of Youth for Christ.

MOUNT PETERS (2850 m) This mountain 80 km northwest of Banff was named by Richard W. Cautley (of Mount Cautley fame). Cautley named this mountain in 1928 after Frederick H. Peters, O.B.E., D.L.S. Peters was a distinguished engineer and served as surveyor general of Canada.

MOUNT PHILLIPS (3249 m) This mountain was named after Donald "Curly" Phillips. He was a well-known guide in the area. Mount Phillips is about 86 km west-northwest of Jasper.

M

MOUNT PILKINGTON (3285 m) This mountain 115 km northwest of Banff was named after Charles Pilkington. He was president of the Alpine Club of London.

MOUNT PUTNIK (2940 m) This mountain 70 km west of Turner Valley was named after Field Marshal R. Putnik. This Serbian Army officer was the Serbian war minister during World War I.

MOUNT QUEEN ELIZABETH (2850 m) This mountain was named in 1918 after Queen Elizabeth of Belgium, the consort of Belgium's King Albert I. Mount Queen Elizabeth is about 80 km west of Turner Valley.

MOUNT QUINCY (3150 m) This mountain about 65 km southeast of Jasper was named after Lucius Quincy Coleman. He was a rancher in the area.

MOUNT QUIRK (1890 m) This mountain northwest of Turner Valley was named after local rancher John Quirk. (The Kew Ridge southeast of Mount Quirk was named after John Quirk's "Kew Ranch" and his cattle brand, a "Q.")

MOUNT RAE (3218 m) This mountain was named after Dr. John Rae (1813–93). He was a Scottish explorer and served as a surgeon on a Hudson's Bay Company ship in 1833. His career included surveying a proposed telegraph line from the Red River Settlement to the Pacific Coast. Rae also took part in the search for the ships of Franklin's second Arctic expedition.

MOUNT REMUS (2688 m) Mount Remus is about 60 km west-southwest of Calgary. (see Mount Romulus)

MOUNT RHONDDA (3055 m) This mountain was named after David Alfred Thomas, First Viscount Baron Rhondda. He was a businessman and served as a British MP. Mount Rhondda is about 85 km northwest of Banff.

MOUNT RICHARDS (2377 m) This mountain was named after Admiral G.R. Richards. He was a commissioner of the 1856–63 British Boundary Commission. Mount Richards is about 55 km south of Pincher Creek.

MOUNT RICHARDSON (3086 m) This mountain was named after Sir John Richardson. He was a surgeon and naturalist on Sir Franklin's Arctic expeditions of 1819 and 1825. Mount Richardson is approximately 55 km northwest of Banff.

MOUNT ROBERTSON (3194 m) This mountain was named after Sir William Robert Robertson. He was a British field marshal during World War I. Mount Robertson is about 75 km west of Turner Valley.

MOUNT ROMULUS (2832 m) This mountain took its name from Romulus, the legendary founder and first king of Rome. According to Roman mythology, Remus and Romulus were twin sons of Rhea Silvia and the god Mars. The boys were suckled by a wolf. When the twins reached adulthood, Remus was slain, and Romulus went on to reign alone, founding the city of Rome. Mount Romulus, about 60 km west-southwest of Calgary, is adjacent to its "twin" Mount Remus, which is approximately the same height.

M

MOUNT ROSS COX (2994 m) This mountain 46 km south of Jasper was named after Ross Cox. He was first employed as a fur trader with Astor's Pacific Fur Company. When that company was bought by the North West Company in 1813, Cox began working for the NWC. In 1817, he travelled up the Columbia River and struck out to cross Canada. He crossed the Athabasca Pass and eventually arrived in Montréal. (see Astoria Pass)

MOUNT ROWE (2452 m) This mountain just west of Waterton Lakes National Park was named after Lieutenant V.F. Rowe. He was the surveying officer for the North

American Boundary Commission (1872–74). The Commission defined the Canada–U.S. border from the Lake of the Woods to the Rocky Mountains.

MOUNT RUNDLE (2846 m) This landmark of Banff was named in 1858 by Sir James Hector of the Palliser Expedition. He named it after Reverend Robert T. Rundle, a Methodist missionary who arrived at Fort Edmonton in 1840. Rundle spent much time in northern and southern parts of the province, though he had limited success establishing missions. Rundle worked extensively with the Cree and was a master of the Cree language. He returned to England in 1848.

MOUNT RUSSELL (2819 m) This mountain about 60 km east of Jasper was named after a pioneer prospector.

MOUNT RUTHERFORD (2847 m) This mountain 40 km northwest of Jasper was named after the first premier of Alberta, Alexander Cameron Rutherford.

MORE ABOUT A.C. RUTHERFORD… *A.C. Rutherford practised law in Ontario before moving west in 1895. He immediately became involved in the politics of the North-West Territories. When Alberta gained provincial status in 1905, Rutherford was named acting premier of the province by Lieutenant-Governor G.H.V. Bulyea. Rutherford confirmed his hold on the premiership two months later in a provincial election, when his Liberal party won almost all of the 25 seats. In Alberta's second provincial election (in 1909), Rutherford's Liberal government again won a big majority. Rutherford resigned as premier a year later over the Alberta and Great Waterways Railway scandal. A royal commission set up to investigate what was described as a generous deal between the province and the railway cleared Rutherford of any wrongdoing but also noted that he failed to act in the best interest of Alberta. After the scandal, Rutherford ran for re-election as an MLA but was not* *elected. He was appointed chancellor of the University of Alberta in 1927 and served in that position until his death in 1941 at the age of 84. Rutherford said his finest achievement as premier was the establishment of the University of Alberta.*

MOUNT SARBACH (3155 m) This mountain was named after Peter Sarbach. He was the first Swiss guide in Canada and, in 1897, was among the group that first climbed this mountain. Mount Sarbach is about 115 km northwest of Banff.

MOUNT SARRAIL (3170 m) This mountain 65 km west-southwest of Turner Valley was named after General Maurice Paul E. Sarrail. He commanded the French Third Army in World War I.

MOUNT SCOTT (3300 m) This mountain was named in honour of Captain Robert F. Scott. He led two Antarctic expeditions in the early 1900s. Mount Scott is 47 km south of Jasper.

MOUNT SCRIMGER (2755 m) This mountain was named after a Canadian war hero. During World War I, Captain Francis A.C. Scrimger, V.C., M.D. showed exceptional courage in caring for the wounded. Mount Scrimger is 60 km southwest of Turner Valley.

MOUNT SECORD (2679 m) This mountain near the Crowsnest Pass was named after Richard Secord (1860–1935) in recognition of his contribution to the development of western Canada. Secord served on the North-West Territoritorial Legislative Assembly. He helped arrange Edmonton's portion of the financing for the 1900 Low Level Bridge, the first bridge across the North Saskatchewan River. In 1903, he put up money for the Conservative *Edmonton Journal* to compete with the Liberal *Edmonton Bulletin*.

M

MOUNT SHARK (2786 m) This mountain 90 km west-southwest of Calgary took its name from a destroyer that was sunk during the 1916 Battle of Jutland.

MOUNT SIR DOUGLAS (3589 m) This mountain 75 km west of Turner Valley was named in 1918 after Field Marshal Sir Douglas Haig, K.T., G.C.B., commander-in-chief of the British armies in France during World War I.

MOUNT SIR HAROLD MITCHELL (2499 m) This mountain 92 km southwest of Edson was named in 1983 after Sir Harold Mitchell. Mitchell had a long association with the coal-mining industry.

MOUNT SKENE (3060 m) This mountain was named after Peter Skene Ogden. He was a fur trader for the North West Company and became a chief factor with the Hudson's Bay Company. Mount Skene is about 110 km northwest of Banff.

MOUNT SMITH-DORRIEN (3155 m) This mountain 70 km west of Turner Valley was named after British General Sir Horace Lockwood Smith-Dorrien. Smith-Dorrien fought in the Zulu and Boer wars and was a British army commander in World War I.

MOUNT SMUTS (2938 m) This mountain about 90 km west-southwest of Calgary was named after General Jan C. Smuts. During the Boer War, he commanded Boer rebels fighting against the British army. He served as prime minister of the Union of South Africa in the 1920s and during World War II.

MOUNT SOLOMON (1585 m) This mountain was named after Solomon Caraconté. He was one of the first Iroquois in the Jasper area. Mount Solomon is near Hinton.

MOUNT SOUTHESK (3125 m) This mountain was named after Sir James Carnegie, Ninth Earl of Southesk. He came to Canada in 1859 and led the "Southesk party" that conducted extensive exploration of the Rocky Mountains and the foothills. While exploring and travelling, Southesk often read Shakespeare. The earl recounted his travels in the book *Saskatchewan and the Rocky Mountains.* Mount Southesk is about 55 km east-southeast of Jasper.

MOUNT SPARROWHAWK (3121 m) This mountain about 80 km west of Calgary was named after a destroyer that took part in the 1916 Battle of Jutland.

MOUNT SPRING-RICE (3275 m) This mountain was named after Sir Cecil Arthur Spring-Rice, K.C.M.G. He was a British diplomat. Mount Spring-Rice is about 110 km southeast of Jasper.

MOUNT ST. BRIDE (3315 m) This mountain near Mount Douglas was named after the patron saint of the Douglas family. It is located about 55 km northwest of Banff.

MOUNT STELFOX (2134 m) This mountain about 110 km west-southwest of Rocky Mountain House was named after Henry Stelfox. He was a pioneer of the area.

MOUNT STEWART (3312 m) This mountain was named after Louis B. Stewart. He was a professor of Surveying and Geodesy at the University of Toronto. Mount Stewart is 105 km southeast of Jasper.

MOUNT STRACHAN (2682 m) This mountain was named after Lieutenant Henry Strachan, V.C. (1889–1917). Strachan came to Canada from Scotland in the early 1900s, and during World War I, he joined the Canadian army. Lt. Strachan was awarded the Victoria Cross for leading his squadron of cavalry through a line of enemy soldiers firing machine guns and then charging a cannon crew and killing seven of the crew with his sword. Mount Strachan is about 49 km southwest of Turner Valley.

M

MOUNT STRAHAN (3060 m) This mountain was named after Dr. Aubrey Strahan, the director of the Geological Survey of Great Britain. Mount Strahan is approximately 100 km northwest of Banff.

MOUNT STRANGE (2887 m) This mountain was named after Major General T. Bland Strange. During his military career, he served in both the British and Canadian military. In 1881, Strange left the Canadian army and set up the Military Colonization Company's ranch in southern Alberta. During the 1885 Riel Rebellion, he joined the Canadian army, commanding the Alberta Field Force. The troops of his command were rushed from the CPR train station at Calgary to the small settlement of Edmonton, thought to be threatened, and then, after the rebellion was subdued, were sent in pursuit of groups of fleeing Natives.

MOUNT SULLIVAN (2975 m) This mountain about 120 km northwest of Banff was named after John W. Sullivan. He was the secretary and astronomical observer on the Palliser Expedition.

MOUNT SWENSEN (2347 m) This mountain was named after Flying Officer Stanley P. Swensen. Swensen's name is listed on the Honour Roll of Canadians who died in the World War II Battle of Britain. Mount Swensen is 80 km northwest of Jasper.

MOUNT SYNGE (2972 m) This mountain about 105 km northwest of Banff was named after Captain Millington H. Synge of the Royal Engineers. A soldier and map-maker, he drew the route through the Rockies that was later followed by the Canadian Pacific Railway.

MOUNT TALBOT (2373 m) This mountain was named after Peter Talbot (1854–1919). He was a member of the Legislative Assembly of the North-West Territories in the early 1900s, then an MP, and in 1905 was appointed to the Senate. Mount Talbot is 49 km southwest of Grande Cache.

MOUNT TECUMSEH (2549 m) This mountain near Coleman was named after a Shawnee chief. Tecumseh (Shooting Star) fought alongside Sir Isaac Brock against U.S. forces in the War of 1812.

MOUNT TEKARRA (2688 m) This mountain near Jasper was named after an Iroquois hunter.

MOUNT TEMPLE (3543 m) This mountain about 50 km northwest of Banff was named in 1884 after Sir Richard Temple. He was president of the Economic Science and Statistics section of the British Association, a group of scholars and scientists. In 1884, he led the British Association's excursion to the Canadian Rockies.

MOUNT THOMPSON (3084 m) This mountain 85 km northwest of Banff was named after C.S. Thompson. He was a member of the Appalachian Mountain Club and an avid mountaineer.

MOUNT THORNTON (2752 m) This mountain 33 km north-northwest of Jasper was named after Sir Henry Thornton. He was president of the Canadian National Railway from 1922 to 1933.

MOUNT TOMA (2760 m) This mountain took its name from an Iroquois canoeman with the Southesk party. The group, led by James Carnegie, Ninth Earl of Southesk, conducted extensive exploration of the Rocky Mountains and foothills. Mount Toma is about 58 km east-southeast of Jasper.

MOUNT TORRENS (2220 m) This mountain 75 km northwest of Grande Cache took its name from Sir Robert R. Torrens. He was the first premier of South Australia and, in the mid-1800s, developed the Torrens System of Land Titles,

M

later used in the Canadian West. The name of the mountain was suggested by Richard W. Cautley, of the Alberta–British Columbia Boundary Commission of 1918–24.

MOUNT TRUTCH (3258 m) This mountain about 110 km northwest of Banff was named after Sir Joseph Trutch. He was the first lieutenant-governor of British Columbia, from 1871 to 1876.

MOUNT TURBULENT (2813 m) This mountain took its name from a destroyer engaged in the 1916 Battle of Jutland. Mount Turbulent is about 90 km west of Calgary.

MOUNT TURNER (2813 m) This mountain, about 90 km west of Calgary, was named after Lieutenant-General Sir Richard E. Turner, K.C.M.G., K.C.B., D.S.O. He commanded Canadian troops during World War I.

MOUNT TUZO (3246 m) This mountain about 50 km northwest of Banff was named after Henrietta Tuzo. She was the first to climb this mountain. Mount Tuzo is number seven of the peaks that line The Valley of the Ten Peaks.

MOUNT TYRRELL (2755 m) This mountain was named after Joseph B. Tyrrell (1858–1957). He was involved in various surveys of the Rockies. In 1884, while exploring the Red Deer River valley for the Canadian Geological Commission, he found the first of the many dinosaur fossils that would be found in The Badlands there. Mount Tyrrell is 60 km northwest of Banff. (see Drumheller)

MOUNT TYRWHITT (2874 m) This mountain about 55 km west-southwest of Turner Valley was named after Rear Admiral Sir Reginald Y. Tyrwhitt. He commanded British warships during World War I.

MOUNT UNWIN (3268 m) This mountain was named after Sidney J. Unwin. He was a guide to Mary Schäffer, the first white woman to venture into parts of the Rockies and the first to see Maligne Lake. Mount Unwin is about 47 km southeast of Jasper. (see Maligne Lake)

MOUNT VICTORIA (3464 m) This mountain 60 km west-northwest of Banff was named in honour of Queen Victoria (1819–1901).

MOUNT WALKER (3303 m) This mountain about 110 km northwest of Banff was named after Horace Walker, president of the Alpine Club in London, England.

MOUNT WARSPITE (2819 m) This mountain took its name from the British cruiser HMS *Warspite*, which took part in the 1916 Battle of Jutland. Mount Warspite is about 65 km west of Turner Valley.

MOUNT WEED (3080 m) This mountain was named after G.M. Weed. He was a member of the Appalachian Mountain Club of Boston and made many first ascents in the Rocky Mountains. Mount Weed is 90 km northwest of Banff.

MOUNT WEISS (3090 m) This mountain was named after Joe Weiss. After coming from Switzerland in 1921, Weiss later settled in Jasper, where he acted as a guide and photographer. His photographic work is internationally known. Mount Weiss is 67 km south-southeast of Jasper.

MOUNT WHITEAVES (3150 m) This mountain 105 km northwest of Banff was named after palaeontologist Joseph F. Whiteaves. He was one of the original Fellows of the Royal Society of Canada.

MOUNT WHYTE (2983 m) This mountain northwest of Banff was named after Sir William M. Whyte. He worked for the Grand Trunk Railway and was vice-president of the Canadian Pacific Railway.

M

MOUNT WILCOX (2884 m) This mountain was named after Walter D. Wilcox (see Wilcox Pass). Mount Wilcox is located about 90 km southeast of Jasper.

MOUNT WILLIAM BOOTH (2728 m) This mountain about 115 km northwest of Banff was named after the founder of the Salvation Army, William Booth.

MOUNT WILSON (3260 m) This mountain about 130 km southeast of Jasper was named after Tom E. Wilson. He was a well-known Rocky Mountain guide, trapper and homesteader in the late 1800s.

MOUNT ZENGEL (2560 m) This mountain took its name from Sergeant Raphael L. Zengel, V.C., M.M. Zengel (1894–?) was born in the United States and moved to Rocky Mountain House. During World War I, he enlisted in the Canadian Army, and during the fighting in France, he won the Military Medal for taking leadership after the officers of his unit had been killed. Later, he won the Victoria Cross for attacking an enemy machine gun emplacement. Mount Zengel is near Jasper.

MOUNTAIN VIEW This hamlet has a good view of the surrounding landscape and mountains. Mountain View is 83 km southwest of Lethbridge.

MUHIGAN MOUNTAIN (2609 m) This mountain took its name from a Native word for "wolf." Muhigan Mountain is near Jasper.

MULHURST BAY This hamlet was originally named Mulhurst, a combination of the name of its first postmaster, George W. Mulligan, and *hurst*, which is Old English for "hill wood." In 1992, "bay" was added because of the hamlet's location on the shores of a bay of Pigeon Lake. Mulhurst Bay is 43 km east-northeast of Wetaskiwin.

MUMM PEAK (2962 m) This mountain took its name from Arnold L. Mumm. He was the first to climb this mountain and was an active member of the Alpine Club of Canada. Mumm Peak is about 79 km northwest of Jasper.

MUNDARE Pop. 653. This town was named after William Mundare, the area's first railway station agent. Most of the settlers here came from the steppes of Ukraine. Mundare is the home of the Basilian Fathers Museum, which gives a history of Ukrainian settlement in the area and of the Basilians in Canada. Mundare is about 77 km east of Edmonton.

MUNSON Pop. 204. It is believed this village was named after J.A. Munson, a member of a Winnipeg law firm that likely did work for the Canadian National Railway. It is also possible that the village was named after a railway engineer.

MUSIDORA It is thought this hamlet was named after the French hometown of local mail carrier Edvert Robarge. Musidora is near Two Hills.

MYRNAM Pop. 294. The name of this village is the Ukrainian word for "peace to us." Myrnam is about 35 km east-southeast of Two Hills.

MYSTERY LAKE It is uncertain, perhaps even a mystery, how this lake received its name. One account has it that an early settler, F.W. Harris, discovered this lake. On his next trip, he was unable to find the lake to show to his friends—giving the lake its name. The area post office closed in 1970, and the lake has now dried up. Its name continues as the name of the nearby locality. Mystery Lake is about 34 km west of Barrhead.

M

N

NACMINE The name for this hamlet west of Drumheller is a combination of the first letters of the name of the local employer, North American Collieries, and the word "mine."

NAMAO Situated on the banks of the Sturgeon River, this hamlet took its name from the Cree word for "sturgeon." Namao is about 17 km north of Edmonton and is near a huge Canadian Forces base.

NAMPA Pop. 427. This village was named after a community in Idaho. In former times, the Alberta village was known as Tank because of its proximity to a railway water tank. According to one account, the name caused Tank to be confused with the Alberta village of Frank, so a new name for Tank was needed. Store owner Robert Perry Christian, a former Idahoan, suggested the name of his old hometown, which is a Native word meaning "the place." Nampa is 24 km south-southeast of Peace River.

NANGA PARBAT MOUNTAIN (3240) This mountain 110 km northwest of Banff took its name from the name of a Himalayan mountain. *Nanga parbat* translates as "bare mountain."

NANTON Pop. 1665. This town was named after Sir Augustus Meredith Nanton, a prominent Canadian financier. Sir Augustus was involved in various development projects in western Canada and was a partner of the Winnipeg financial firm of Osler, Hammond and Nanton. He also served as managing director of Galt's North Western Coal and Navigation Company and was knighted in 1917 for his efforts in directing the Western Patriotic Fund and Victory Loan campaigns during World War I. Before 1893, the community was known as Mosquito Creek. Nanton is about 65 km south of Calgary. (see Ohaton)

NASSWALD PEAK (2995 m) This peak was named after the Austrian hometown of Conrad Kain, who climbed this peak. Nasswald Peak is situated near Banff.

NEEDLE PEAK (2850 m) This descriptive name refers to the needle-like shape of the mountain's summit. Needle Peak is located 38 km southwest of Jasper.

NEERLANDIA This hamlet was named after the Netherlands, the homeland of the area's early settlers. Neerlandia is near Barrhead.

NEPTUAK MOUNTAIN (3233 m) *Neptuak* is Stoney for "nine." Neptuak Mountain is the ninth mountain adjoining the Valley of the Ten Peaks, about 50 km west-northwest of Banff.

NESTOW This hamlet near Westlock took its name from the Cree word for "brother-in-law." It is not known why this particular name was chosen for the community.

NETOOK The name for this locality is from its Blackfoot place name, *nee-tuck-kis*, meaning "lone pine tree." The name was recorded around 1792 by surveyor-mapmaker Peter Fidler when he noted in his journal the presence of a tall, single pine tree near a point of woods. Explorer-mapmaker David Thompson, Fidler's rival, also noted that Natives made offerings in the location of this pine. Netook is close to Olds and is unrelated to Lone Pine near Mayerthorpe.

NEVIS This hamlet near Stettler was named after the nearby Ben Nevis Coal Mine. It is likely the mine's name was taken from Ben Nevis, Scotland.

NEW BRIGDEN This hamlet was named after Brigden, Ontario, the former home of many of the settlers who moved to this part of Alberta. New Brigden is 40 km north of Oyen.

NEW DAYTON This hamlet took its name from Dayton, Ohio. It was so named by David Hunter, after his hometown. New Dayton is about 45 km southeast of Lethbridge.

NEW NORWAY Pop. 270. This village took its name from the homeland of many settlers in the area. The name "Norway" means "northern way," referring to the country's northern latitude. New Norway is near Camrose.

NEW SAREPTA Pop. 359. There are different theories of how this village southeast of Edmonton was named. Some claim it was named after a city near Biblical Sidon (the present-day village of Sarafand), while others say it was named after a Russian settlement. New Sarepta is about 40 km southeast of Edmonton.

NEWBROOK This hamlet was so named because of its proximity to a creek (or brook). Newbrook is about 40 km northwest of Smoky Lake.

NEWMAN PEAK (2621 m) This mountain was named after the famous English naturalist Edward Newman. He published many books on plants, birds and insects. Newman Peak is near Waterton Lakes National Park.

NIGHTINGALE This hamlet was named in honour of Florence Nightingale, an English nurse celebrated for her selfless work among the wounded in the Crimean War (1854–55). She was the first women to receive the Order of Merit and is recognized as the founder of trained professional nursing. Nightingale is about 50 km east-northeast of Calgary.

NISKU This hamlet took its name for the Cree word for "wild goose." Nisku is south of Edmonton.

NITON Pop. 85. The name for this hamlet about 45 km east of Edson is a reverse spelling of "not in," an apparent reference to the station agent who was often not at his post.

NITON JUNCTION Pop. 100. This hamlet took its name from its nearby sister community of Niton.

NOBLEFORD Pop. 558. This village near Lethbridge was named after Charles S. Noble. Nobleford is about 22 km northwest of Lethbridge.

MORE ABOUT CHARLES NOBLE... *Charles Noble was the owner of a large farming operation and the inventor of the Noble Blade Cultivator. In the early 1900s, Noble bought about 2000 hectares of land near Lethbridge and later expanded the operation to 35,000 hectares. But Noble's fortunes declined when wheat prices fell after World War I, and he nearly went out of business. In response, Noble developed new conservation and erosion-control techniques, including his Noble Blade Cultivator. The Noble Blade Cultivator was a special plow that could be used with less disruption to the topsoil and caused less moisture loss from the soil. The implement became widely used and made Noble world famous. It helped save his farm.*

N

NOJACK The name was derived from the slang for "no money." As one account has it, this hamlet was named by a couple of entrepreneurs who did not have enough money to open a business at this location. Another story relates to a worker who proposed marriage a number of times to a local girl, only to be told "No, Jack."

NORAL It is thought the name for this hamlet is a contraction of "Northern Alberta." Noral is near Lac La Biche.

NORDEGG Pop. 400 (estimated). This hamlet was named after Martin Nordegg, a German immigrant and successful businessman. Shortly after his arrival in Canada in 1906, Nordegg constructed a coal mine, Brazeau Collieries, in the Alberta foothills. To house his mineworkers, he established Nordegg, a "company town." During World War I, his assets, including the mine, were confiscated by the Canadian government on the grounds that he was an enemy of the country. His holdings were later returned to him, and Nordegg went on to write a book entitled *The Possibilities of Canada are Truly Great*. Nordegg is about 155 km northwest of Red Deer.

NORTH SASKATCHEWAN RIVER This river is the northern branch of the 1939-km-long Saskatchewan River. The North Saskatchewan River starts at the Columbia Icefield, in particular the Saskatchewan Glacier, and crosses Alberta. In Saskatchewan, it is joined by the 1392-km-long South Saskatchewan River. Its waters cross several lakes in Saskatchewan and Manitoba before the Nelson River carries them to Hudson Bay. One of the great rivers of the prairies, it took the name from its Cree name *kis-is-ska-tche-wan*, meaning "swift current."

NOTIKEWIN This hamlet in northern Alberta near Manning took its name from the nearby Notikewin River. It was previously known as Battle River, but postal officials requested the name be changed to avoid duplication of the Battle River name already in use in central Alberta. Notikewin is a rough approximation of the Native place name *Notenaygewan*, meaning "battle river." It denotes a battle that took place on this location between the Cree and Beaver.

O

OBED Pop. 34. This locality and a nearby lake were named after Lieutenant Colonel John Obed Smith. He served in various government positions with the Manitoba and federal governments. Obed is about 51 km west of Edson. At 1164 metres, it is the highest point on the Yellowhead Highway as it winds through the Rockies, the Yellowhead Pass being lower. (see Yellowhead Pass)

OBSERVATION PEAK (3147 m) The name of this mountain refers to the view Rev. C.L. Noyes saw when he climbed the mountain in the late 1800s. Observation Peak is about 90 km northwest of Banff.

OHATON Pop. 142. This hamlet took its name from a combination of parts of the name Osler, Hammond & Nanton, a leading Winnipeg financial firm that backed western Canadian development, land and railway projects. Ohaton is near Camrose. (see Nanton)

OKOTOKS Pop. 9953. It is likely the name for this town comes from the Blackfoot word *okatok*, meaning "rock." It refers to a large glacial boulder near the town that, by some accounts, is the largest erratic in the world, weighing in at some 18,000 tonnes. When incorporated in 1904, Okotoks was a lumber and oil center. Today, Okotoks, about 34 km south of Calgary, is more of a rural recreational centre and a commuter community of Calgary.

OKOTOKS MOUNTAIN (1762 m) Okotoks Mountain is located about 50 km southwest of Okotoks near the town of Turner Valley. This mountain took its name from the Blackfoot word for "rock."

OLDMAN RIVER This river took its name from the mythical Cree character *Wi-suk-i-shak*, meaning "Old Man," who had supernatural abilities. About 85 km east of Lethbridge, the Oldman River joins the Bow River to form the South Saskatchewan River.

OLDHORN MOUNTAIN (3000 m) This mountain was named for its shape, which resembles a horn. Oldhorn Mountain is near Jasper.

OLDS Pop. 5815. This town was named after George Olds, a Canadian Pacific Railway traffic manager. The Olds area was previously known as Lone Pine after the Lone Pine stopping place on the Calgary-Edmonton Trail. (This name survives in the name of the nearby locality Netook.(see Netook)) When the Calgary & Edmonton Railway was built through the area around 1891, the area took the name Sixth Siding. The growing railway centre then took the name Hay City to reflect the centre's trade in cattle feed. In 1905, when Hay City was about to incorporate as a town, a new name, Olds, was chosen. An agricultural centre, the town is the home of the Olds Agricultural College, a leader in agricultural research. Olds is 58 km southwest of Red Deer.

ONEFOUR This locality was so named by settlers because they thought the area was in Township One, Range Four, west of the Fourth Meridian, putting it within 10 km of the Canada–U.S. border. However, they later learned its correct location was Section 15 in Township Two, Range Four, west of the Fourth Meridian, about 15 km north of the border—but the name was not changed. Onefour is 100 km south of Medicine Hat.

ONOWAY Pop. 788. There are different versions of how this village was named. Perhaps the name is a Chipewyan place name for "fair field," or perhaps the name was taken from Longfellow's poem "Hiawatha," in which a singer begins a canto with "onaway," meaning "awake." Onoway is about 50 km northwest of Edmonton.

OPAL It is not certain how this hamlet received its name. Opal is about 50 km north-northeast of Edmonton.

OPAL HILLS These hills about 40 km southeast of Jasper are named for their beautiful colouring. They are blue in the morning mists, and green and yellow when the sun shines on them.

OPPY MOUNTAIN (3335 m) This mountain was named after a French village to commemorate the fighting that occurred there during World War I. Oppy Mountain is about 140 km northwest of Banff.

ORTON This hamlet was named after Josiah Orr, a pioneer in the district and the community's first postmaster. Orton is about 32 km west of Lethbridge.

OTUSKWAN PEAK (2530 m) The descriptive name for this mountain comes from the Cree word for "elbow." Otuskwan Peak is about 40 km north of Banff.

OVERTURN MOUNTAIN (2560 m) This is a descriptive name for the rock formations along the ridges of this mountain that appear to have been turned over. Overturn Mountain is 43 km south-southwest of Hinton.

OYEN Pop. 1075. This town was named after Andrew Oyen, a Norwegian settler. Oyen is located about 156 km east of Drumheller.

OZADA This locality took its name from the Stoney word for "the forks of the river." Ozada is located where the Kananaskis River flows into the Bow River, about 55 km west of Calgary.

P

PADDLE PRAIRIE This hamlet was named by white settlers who saw canoes and paddles abandoned among trees in the area. Prior to the time of the settlers' arrival, Paddle Prairie had been a swampy area and had been inhabited by Beaver and Slavey people who used canoes and paddles to get around. When the area dried up, the Natives moved on, leaving their canoes and paddles behind. Paddle Prairie is about 75 km southwest of High Level.

PADDLE PRAIRIE MÉTIS SETTLEMENT This settlement, formerly known as the Keg River Metis Colony, was renamed in 1990. The new name was chosen because the settlement is located in the Paddle Prairie area.

PAKAKOS MOUNTAIN (2440 m) This mountain near Banff took its name from the Native word that means the "spirit of a flying skeleton." The name was selected from suggestions made by elementary schoolchildren in a contest held during the International Year of the Child (1979).

PALISADE, THE This ridge near Jasper was named for its resemblance to an enclosure or palisade.

PALLISER PASS Palliser Pass is located 80 km west of Turner Valley. This pass was named after Captain John Palliser, the leader of the Palliser Expedition. (see Palliser Range)

MORE ABOUT PALLISER EXPEDITION…*Sponsored by the British Colonial Office, the Palliser Expedition (1857–60) set out to determine whether western Canada was suitable for settlement, whether there were suitable passes through the Rocky Mountains and whether the territory could be linked with other British possessions,* *in particular, the colonies along the St. Lawrence River and the Pacific coast. They explored a vast area that stretched between the 49th Parallel and the North Saskatchewan River, from the Red River to the Rocky Mountains. Palliser had a good team to assist him in this mammoth undertaking, which gleaned astronomical, geological and magnetic data, as well as information concerning the area's inhabitants, flora and fauna. The team included:*

- **Sir James Hector** *(geologist and medical doctor), the name-sake of Mount Hector,*
- **Eugène Bourgeau** *(botanist), the namesake of Mount Bourgeau,*
- **Lieutenant Thomas Blakiston** *(magnetic observer), the namesake of Mount Blakiston, and*
- **John Sullivan** *(astronomical observer), the namesake of Mount Sullivan.*

PALLISER RANGE This mountain range located near Banff was named after Captain John Palliser.

MORE ABOUT JOHN PALLISER... *John Palliser, the son of an Irish nobleman, preferred a life of adventure to the society life of upper-class England. In the 1840s, Palliser hunted along the Upper Missouri before he came up with the idea of exploring the Canadian Prairies. At first, his western Canadian expedition was going to be a one-man expedition that Palliser was going to fund himself. However, Palliser convinced the Colonial Office that it was a good idea for the British government to find out first-hand about the area instead of relying on information supplied by the Hudson's Bay Company. (The company, with its fur trade monopoly, had a vested interest in the territory). Palliser's appeal was supported by the fact that the United States was funding western expeditions that occasionally crossed into British territory. In 1857, the British government officially approved the expedition and promised financial support*

P

on the condition that Palliser was joined by experts who would collect botanical, magnetic, geographic and astronomical data. In 1857, the team left England, and three years later it concluded its exploration, having gathered a large amount of information. This information was a major step forward in preserving western Canada as British territory. After this expedition, Palliser was involved in confidential missions to the Caribbean and to the Confederate States, and he explored parts of Russia.

PALU MOUNTAIN (2929 m) This mountain was named after a mountain in Switzerland. Palu Mountain is located about 87 km northwest of Jasper.

PANGMAN PEAK (3473 m) This mountain was named after Peter Pangman. He was an early fur trader and became a partner in the North West Company in 1787. Pangman Peak is 115 km northwest of Banff.

PARADISE VALLEY This sun-flooded valley about 50 km west-northwest of Banff provides contrasts of streams, woods and open country.

PARADISE VALLEY Pop. 141. This village northeast of Wainwright was named by early U.S. settler Frank Henton. The pastoral landscape reminded him of the rolling prairie and poplar bluffs found in his home state of Washington. (It is not related to Paradise Valley, listed above.)

PARAGON PEAK (3030 m) This mountain was named for its majestic appearance and impressive peak. Paragon Peak is near Jasper.

PARKLAND The name for this hamlet about 75 km south of Calgary is similar to the name of W.J. Parkhill, a pioneer resident of the area. At first the area bore his name directly, but its post office could not carry the name Parkhill because the name was already in use elsewhere.

PARLBY CREEK The name for this creek was in use as early as 1894. The creek was apparently named for Walter and Edward Parlby, early settlers in the Alix area. The Parlby name is best remembered for Irene Parlby, Walter's wife and the first woman cabinet minister in Alberta. She was a cabinet minister in the United Farmers of Alberta government (1921–35). (see Alix)

PASQUE MOUNTAIN (2541 m) This mountain took its name from the large numbers of pasque flowers found near its summit. Pasque Mountain is located about 60 km southwest of Turner Valley.

PATRICIA During World War I, this hamlet was named after Princess Patricia of Connaught (1886–1972). She was a granddaughter of Queen Victoria and the daughter of the Duke of Connaught, who served as governor general from 1911 to 1916. Princess Patricia served as honorary colonel of the Princess Patricia's Canadian Light Infantry from 1914 until her death. Patricia is about 98 km northwest of Medicine Hat. (see Empress)

MORE ABOUT PRINCESS PATRICIA'S CANADIAN LIGHT INFANTRY...
The "Pats," as Princess Patricia's Canadian Light Infantry are known, was the first Canadian unit to serve in World War I. The first and most famous battle for the Regiment was Frezenburg in 1915. The "Pats" also fought at Passchendaele, Ypres and Vimy Ridge. They also served in World War II (in Italy and Northwest Europe) and in the Korean War.

P

MORE ABOUT PATRICIA...*Located near Patricia in Dinosaur Provincial Park is a satellite field station of Drumheller's Royal Tyrrell Museum. The station contains a number of fossils of dinosaurs and other animals from the Cretaceous period. About 70,000 to 80,000 tourists visit the field station each year. Most visitors come during July and August.*

PEACE-ATHABASCA DELTA About 211 km north of Fort McMurray, this large freshwater delta actually contains three deltas, that of the Athabasca, the Peace and the Birch rivers at the west end of Lake Athabasca.

PEACE RIVER This river is 1923 km long. It starts at Williston Lake in BC, cuts through the Rockies and traverses northern Alberta to drain into the Slave River, which carries its waters to the Mackenzie River and on to the Arctic Ocean. Peace River was named after Peace Point, a riverside locality about 80 km upstream from Lake Athabasca. Peace Point is the place where the Cree and Beaver settled a territorial dispute and established peace in the late 1700s.

PEACE RIVER Pop. 6536. This town is situated where the Smoky River flows into the Peace. The Hudson's Bay Company built a trading post here in 1818. St. Mary's House was the first post to be established in Peace River country. The settlement that grew there was known as Peace River Crossing, and a community on the east bank of the Peace was called Peace River Landing Settlement. The town of Peace River now includes both of these settlements. In addition to serving local farmers, Peace River serves as a distribution centre for the North. Peace River is about 152 km northeast of Grande Prairie.

MORE ABOUT PEACE RIVER... *Peace River was the home of "Twelve-Foot" Davis, a local folk hero who struck it big during the Cariboo gold rush in BC by staking a claim on a thin, four-metre-wide strip of land between two successful gold mines. By the way, H.F. Davis (1820–93) was a short person, only about 157 cm tall. He opened trading posts in the Peace River area after moving there in 1886.*

PEACE HILLS These hills near Wetaskiwin mark the site where Cree and Blackfoot made peace around 1867. (see Wetaskiwin)

PEERLESS LAKE This hamlet took its name from nearby Peerless Lake, which was named to reflect the "peerless" pristine quality of its blue water. Peerless Lake is about 156 km north of Slave Lake.

PEERS This hamlet near Edson was named after the family name of Marion Peers Davidson. She was the mother of Sir Charles Peers Davidson (1841–1929), a chief justice in the Superior Court of Québec in the early 1900s.

PENHOLD Pop. 1625. This town took its name from a pen accidentally dropping on a map. When the nib of the pen stuck in the map, the paper seemed to have a good hold on the pen. A "eureka moment" happened, and the name Penhold came to mind for the group trying to name this community. Penhold is near Red Deer.

PEORIA It is believed this hamlet was named after a city of the same name in Illinois. The hamlet was likely named by settlers who came from the U.S. state. Peoria is about 35 km northeast of Grande Prairie.

PEYTO PEAK (2970 m) This mountain peak, like nearby Peyto Glacier, was named after Bill Peyto. He was reputed to be one of the best guides in the Rocky Mountains. He came to Canada from England in the late 1800s. Before developing his talents as a guide and outfitter, Peyto homesteaded and worked on the railway. Peyto Peak is 90 km northwest of Banff. (see Trapper Peak)

PHARAOH PEAKS (2711 m) This mountain peak took its name from its resemblance to Egyptian mummies. Pharaoh Peaks is near Banff.

PHILOMENA Historical records state this hamlet was named after a nearby lake. However, no lake with that name has been found. Philomena is about 40 km northeast of Lac La Biche.

P

PIBROCH This hamlet, originally a Scottish settlement, took its name from the Scottish word for "bagpipe music." Pibroch, near Westlock, was made a village in 1910 and then a municipal district in 1912. It is now only a hamlet. Pibroch was formerly named Debney, after a railway engineer.

PICKARDVILLE This hamlet south of Westlock was named for its first postmaster, William Pickard. The post office opened here in 1907.

PICTURE BUTTE Pop. 1669. This town took its name from a nearby hill that had a number of Native spiritual icons on its top. The icons took the form of pictures and patterns made with small stones. These pictures are now gone, because the earth at the top of Picture Butte was removed and used to repair the town's streets. Picture Butte is 20 km north of Lethbridge.

PIGEON MOUNTAIN (2394 m) This mountain took its name from the flocks of wild pigeons seen in the area. Pigeon Mountain is near Canmore.

PINCHER CREEK Pop. 3659. This town about 85 km west-southwest of Lethbridge took its name from the nearby Pincher Creek. The creek took its name from a historic pair of pincers, pincer later becoming pincher. There are different stories concerning the pincers. One story suggests that a group of prospectors lost the pincers at this creek in the 1860s, which were then found, old and rusted, by a detachment of the North-West Mounted Police who were setting up a post here in the 1870s. Another story proposes that U.S. prospectors were attacked by Natives in the area. Pincers belonging to one of the prospectors were found at one of their campsites. Pincher Creek is a tributary of the Highwood River, and the Natives referred to this creek as *unuk-spitzee* meaning "little highwood." Similar to the trees growing along Highwood River (which

P

gave us the name of the town of High River), trees growing on the banks of Pincher Creek are visible for a great
distance.

PINNACLE MOUNTAIN (3067 m) This is a descriptive
name for this mountain located about 50 km west-
northwest of Banff.

PLAMONDON Pop. 302. This village near Lac La Biche was
named after Joseph Plamondon, its first postmaster. The
Plamondons came to Canada from France in the late
1600s, settling in Québec. Joseph came to Alberta in 1908.
The settlement was first known as Plamondonville, but
the name was later shortened to Plamondon.

PLATEAU MOUNTAIN (2438 m) This mountain 70 km
west-northwest of Claresholm was named for its plateau.

POE This locality was named after the U.S. writer Edgar Allan
Poe. Poe is near Tofield.

POLLOCKVILLE This hamlet was named after an early
homesteader in the area, Robert Pollock. The Canadian
National Railway opened a station here in 1919. Pollockville is 87 km southeast of Drumheller.

P

PONOKA Pop. 6149. This town took its name from the
Blackfoot word *ponokaii*, meaning "elk." The community
on the Calgary & Edmonton Railway was previously
known as Siding 14. Ponoka is about 105 km south of
Edmonton.

POPE'S PEAK (3163 m) This mountain was named in honour of John Henry Pope. He was a federal cabinet minister
in the late 1800s, serving as minister of Agriculture and of
Railways and Canals. Pope's Peak is about 60 km west-
northwest of Banff.

PRAIRIE MOUNTAIN (2210 m) This mountain 45 km west of Calgary took its name from the nearby prairie stretching eastwards from the Rocky Mountains.

PRIDDIS This hamlet was named after an early homesteader, Charles Priddis. Priddis is near Calgary.

PRINCESS MARGARET MOUNTAIN (2515 m) This mountain near Canmore was named after Her Royal Highness Princess Margaret.

PROTECTION MOUNTAIN (2850 m) This mountain separates a beautiful, unnamed valley and the Baker Creek valley. Protection Mountain is 45 km northwest of Banff.

PROVOST Pop. 2045. Provost is the title given to the chief official of a Scottish town. It is equivalent to a mayor of a Canadian town. Why the town of Provost was given this name is unclear. Provost is 105 km south-southwest of Lloydminster.

PROW MOUNTAIN (2858 m) This mountain took its name from its resemblance to the prow of a ship. Prow Mountain is about 55 km northwest of Banff.

PTARMIGAN PEAK (3035 m) This mountain took its name from the large number of ptarmigan found in the area. Ptarmigan Peak is located about 50 km northwest of Banff.

PULSATILLA MOUNTAIN (3035 m) This mountain located 39 km northwest of Banff was named after a mountain plant that grows in the area. Pulsatilla is the name of a subgenus of *Anemones*.

PUNCHBOWL FALLS These falls have eroded the rock at their base to form a smooth "punchbowl." In 1928 Miss M.B. Williams wrote a suitable description of this beautiful spot in Jasper National Park.

Tucked away in a narrow pocket of a valley, which ends in a cul de sac, are the interesting Punchbowl falls. If the gods of the hills indulged in secret wassailing, one could imagine no better place than this secluded and charming spot. The fall is formed by Punchbowl creek which, running along the rocky ledge above, apparently discovered an opening and way of escape over the precipice. Tumbling down in a straight column, as if poured from a beaker, if falls into a rocky bowl, worn smooth and hollowed into lines graceful as a Grecian urn. Gathering here in a pool of jacinth, it spills over the rim and, reaching the valley, turns sharply at right angles to flow down to Athabasca.

Punchbowl Falls are about 35 km southwest of Hinton and about 100 km south of the unrelated Committee Punchbowl.

PURPLE SPRINGS It is believed this hamlet took its name from a nearby spring where purple flowers grew. Another reason for the name could be the fact that the spring water is high in iron content, which makes sunlight shining on it reflect a purple colour. Purple Springs is 67 km east of Lethbridge.

PYRAMID MOUNTAIN (2766 m) This landmark near Jasper took its name from its pyramid shape.

PYRIFORM MOUNTAIN (2621 m) This mountain was named after the scientific term that means "pear-shaped." Pyriform Mountain is about 33 km west of Turner Valley.

P

Q

QUADRA MOUNTAIN (3173 m) This mountain took its name from the four pinnacles at its summit. Quadra Mountain is located 45 km west-northwest of Banff.

QUEEN ELIZABETH RANGES These ranges around Maligne Lake were named to commemorate the coronation of Her Majesty Queen Elizabeth II in 1953. Queen Elizabeth Ranges are about 24 km east of Jasper.

QUEENSTOWN This hamlet was named after Queenstown, Ireland, which has since been renamed Cobh. The hamlet's name was chosen by Captain Dawson, who formed the Canadian Pacific Colonization Company and gathered many settlers from the Irish city. The hamlet's post office opened in 1908. Queenstown is about 85 km southeast of Calgary.

QUOIN, THE (2454 m) The name describes this mountain, which is located as if it was a cornerstone, or quoin, of the Starlight Range. The Quoin is about 70 km northwest of Jasper.

Q

R

RADWAY This former village near Redwater was named after Orland S. Radway, the district's storekeeper and its first postmaster. The post office opened here in 1910. The community was originally called Radway Centre, but its name was later shortened. Radway was dissolved as a village in 1996.

RAINBOW LAKE Pop. 1138. This town took its name from the nearby lake. The lake, known locally as Long Lake, may have been named Rainbow Lake after its shape. Another theory suggests Rainbow Lake got its name through a mix-up with a nearby lake of the same name (which is now known as Basset Lake), which was named for local trapper Rainbow Fournier. The town of Rainbow Lake is a relatively new town serving the needs of the oil industry. The first post office there opened in 1967. Rainbow Lake is about 132 km west of High Level.

RAINIER The early settlers in this hamlet were mostly former residents of the U.S., and the hamlet was named in the early 1900s after Rainier, Washington. The Washington State community was named after British Rear Admiral Peter Rainier (1741–1808). Rainier is approximately 90 km northeast of Lethbridge.

RAJAH, THE (3018 m) This peak took its name from the Hindi word for "king." The Rajah is located about 53 km northwest of Jasper. (see The Ranee)

RALSTON This hamlet was named after Colonel J.L. Ralston, Canada's minister of National Defence during World War II. In 1944, Prime Minister W.L. Mackenzie King forced Ralston's resignation after Ralston repeatedly called for the use of conscripted (drafted) soldiers in the fighting in Europe, a move vehemently opposed by Québecois and other Canadian voting blocks. The hamlet of Ralston is near Medicine Hat, close to the Canadian Forces' Suffield Experimental Station.

RANEE, THE (2939 m) This mountain about 54 km north-west of Jasper took its name from the Hindi word for "queen." It is near The Rajah.

RANFURLY This hamlet took its name from Sir Uchter John Mark Knox, Fifth Earl of Ranfurly, who served as gover-nor of New Zealand. Ranfurly is 27 km east-southeast of Vegreville.

RAYMOND Pop. 3656 This town was named in honour of Raymond Knight. He was the eldest son of Jesse Knight, a prominent Mormon rancher and businessman. In 1901, Jesse Knight built Canada's first sugar factory. He did so after securing a contract with the North Western Coal and Navigation Company to produce sugar beets on approxi-mately 10,000 hectares of land. This enterprise attracted about 1500 people to the area. Raymond Knight is seen by many to be the father of rodeo. In the early 1900s, he mounted a bucking horse and introduced a new sport to North America. Raymond is near Lethbridge.

RAYMOND HILL This 60-metre-tall hill was named after Andrew Raymond, a rancher who homesteaded on the north side of the hill.

RED DEER Pop. 82,971. The Red Deer River flows through this city. The river received its name for the large number of elk in the vicinity. Early Scottish settlers mistook the elk for the red deer found in Scotland, and the name stuck. The Cree place name, *was-ka-sioo*, means "Elk River." In 1882, people began to settle in Red Deer Crossing, where the old Calgary–Edmonton Trail crossed the Red Deer River. The coming of the Canadian Pacific Railway to

Calgary saw increased traffic through the area, and the name Red Deer Crossing was changed to Red Deer. It incorporated as a city in 1913. The land for the community was donated by Rev. Leonard Gaetz. Today, Red Deer relies mostly on the agricultural and oil industry for its economic base.

MORE ABOUT RED DEER... *Within Red Deer's Waskasoo Park is the Kerry Wood Nature Centre. This permanent exhibit shows the formation of the Red Deer Valley and highlights its wildlife and habitats. There are also videos on the river valley's natural history and a hands-on "Discovery Room" for children. The Kerry Wood Nature Centre is next to the 118-hectare Gaetz Lakes Sanctuary, which has as many as 130 species of birds and 25 species of mammals.*

RED WILLOW Pop. 29. The area's red willow trees seem to have inspired the names for both this hamlet and the nearby Red Willow Creek. The original site of this hamlet was about six km from its present location. A post office named Coralynn opened here in 1903. Red Willow is about 17 km northeast of Stettler.

REDAN MOUNTAIN (2560 m) *Redan* is the French word for a salient (protruding) angle. Two of the mountain faces form a salient angle. Redan Mountain is near Jasper.

R

REDCLIFF Pop. 4104. This town's name refers to the red shale outcroppings (red cliffs) along the banks of the South Saskatchewan River. The name for the area was in use long before a town grew up here. Redcliff is near Medicine Hat.

REDLAND This hamlet took its name from the red soil found in the area. The Canadian National Railway opened a station here in 1914. Redland is about 30 km southwest of Drumheller.

REDOUBT MOUNTAIN (2902 m) The name describes the shape of this mountain. A redoubt, in military terms, is an isolated defensive structure. Redoubt Mountain was named in 1908 by A.O. Wheeler and is about 50 km northwest of Banff.

REDWATER Pop. 2053. This town took its name from the nearby Redwater River. The ochre in the riverbed colours the river water red. The river was originally called Vermilion River, but a different Alberta river now uses the name. Redwater is about 45 km northeast of Edmonton. Redwater River flows into the North Saskatchewan River.

RENO Pop. 25. This hamlet was probably named after Reno, Nevada. The U.S. city itself was named after Major General Reno, who was killed in 1862 during the U.S. Civil War. Reno is about 32 km southeast of Peace River.

REPLICA PEAK (2794 m) The origin of the name for this mountain is uncertain, but it is believed this peak resembles another peak. Replica Peak is about 60 km southeast of Jasper.

RICH VALLEY The name for this hamlet near Barrhead is descriptive of its rich soil. This community was previously known as Onion Prairie.

R

RIDGEVALLEY It is believed this hamlet took its name from the nearby Ridge Valley School District. Ridgevalley is about 60 km east of Grande Prairie and became a hamlet in 1992.

RIMBEY Pop. 2106. This town was named after the Rimbey brothers: Sam, Ben and Jim. They were settlers in the district, with Jim serving as the area's first postmaster. With many of the settlers coming from Kansas, the community was once known as Kansas Ridge. Rimbey is about 48 km northeast of Red Deer.

RINGROSE PEAK (3278 m) This mountain was named in 1894 by Samuel E. Allen, of Mount Allen fame. Allen named this mountain after A.E. Ringrose of London, England, who travelled in the Rocky Mountains. Ringrose Peak is about 55 km west-northwest of Banff.

RIVERCOURSE This hamlet south of Lloydminster was named for its proximity to Blackfoot Creek, which probably got its name from the nearby Blackfoot Hills.

RIVERVIEW This hamlet took its name from the view of the North Saskatchewan River seen from the community. Riverview is near Elk Point.

RIVIÈRE QUI BARRE The name for this hamlet are French words that translate as "the river that bars." Lumbermen unable to drive their logs past this point because of shallow water named this locale. Rivière Qui Barre is near Morinville.

ROBSON PASS (1569 m) This pass was named after nearby Mount Robson, which at 3954 m, is the highest peak in the Rockies. It is uncertain after whom this British Columbia peak was named. The manager of Jasper House in 1814, François Décoigne, may have named this mountain after his boss, Colin Robertson, of the Hudson's Bay Company and North West Company. (see Yellowhead Pass)

R

ROCHE BOULE (2204 m) This mountain near Hinton took its name from the shape at its summit. The French word *boule* means "a ball."

ROCHE DE SMET (2539 m) This mountain was named after Pierre-Jean de Smet, a Belgian missionary. Roche de Smet is located about 29 km north of Jasper. (see White Man Pass)

ROCHE JACQUES (2603 m) It is believed this mountain was named after "Old Jacques Cardinal." He was a North

West Company employee. Roche Jacques is about 50 km southwest of Hinton.

ROCHE NOIRE (2878 m) This mountain near Jasper was named for its black summit.

ROCHE RONDE (2138 m) The descriptive name for this mountain is French for "round rock." Roche Ronde is about 40 km north of Jasper.

ROCHE TÊTE (2418 m) This mountain 33 km west of Jasper was named after a blonde trapper with the nickname "Tête Jaune." (see Yellowhead Pass)

ROCHESTER Pop. 107. This hamlet was named after Herbert Rochester, secretary to M.H. MacLeod, a senior executive of the Canadian Northern Railway. The community was previously known as Ideal Flat, but only for a short time. The residents of the community disliked the name given by the railway and insisted it be changed to what they felt was more suitable. Rochester is about 30 km northeast of Westlock.

ROCHFORT BRIDGE This hamlet was named after Cooper Rochfort, a pioneer of the district, and the nearby railway bridge crossing the Paddle River. The 733-metre-long wooden trestle bridge is still in use and is one of the longest wooden trestles in Canada. Rochfort Bridge, formerly known as Wankeville, is near Mayerthorpe.

R

ROCKY MOUNTAIN HOUSE Pop. 6062. This town was named for its proximity to the Rocky Mountains. A fort was first established here in 1799 by the North West Company. Rocky Mountain House closed as a fur-trading centre in 1875, when it was replaced by a post at Calgary.

ROCKY RAPIDS This hamlet took its name from the nearby rapids in the North Saskatchewan River. The post office opened here in 1909. Rocky Rapids is nine km north of Drayton Valley.

ROCKYFORD Pop. 346. The name for this village is descriptive of the nearby rocky ford that was used to cross the Serviceberry Creek. Rocky Ford was named by the First Nations people, and the name was adopted by ranchers and surveyors as the official name of the community. Rockyford is about 42 km southwest of Drumheller.

ROSALIND Pop. 195. This village's name was created by taking parts of the names (with modified spelling) of two nearby school districts: Montrose and East Lynne. This community is southeast of Camrose.

ROSE LYNN This hamlet took its name from the many rosebushes in the area. Rose Lynn is about 70 km east of Drumheller.

ROSEBUD Pop. 88. This hamlet located 25 km southwest of Drumheller took its name from the area's long-used Blackfoot place name meaning "many roses."

MORE ABOUT ROSEBUD...*In 1983, the Rosebud School of the Arts' Dinner Theatre Productions mounted its first live play. Since then, family-entertainment productions have been staged every year, drawing on the talent of students, teachers and professional actors. The Rosebud theatre is a big hit, attracting about 40,000 fans a year.*

R

ROSEDALE Pop. 140. This hamlet was named after the abundance of wild roses found in the area. Rosedale is seven km southeast of Drumheller.

ROSEMARY Pop. 332. This village was named after Rosemary Millicent, a daughter of the Fourth Duke of Sutherland. The duke had a large landholding in southern Alberta. Rosemary is about 135 km northwest of Medicine Hat. (see Millicent)

ROSYTH This hamlet took its name from the famous World War I naval base in Scotland. Rosyth is near Hardisty.

ROUND HILL The name for this hamlet is descriptive of the nearby round-shaped hill. Round Hill is about 22 km northeast of Camrose.

ROWLEY This hamlet took its name from Charles Walsh Rowley, a manager with the Canadian Bank of Commerce. The bank provided financing for the Canadian Northern Railway, which opened a station there. Rowley is southeast of Trochu. (see Rumsey)

ROYALTIES This hamlet near Turner Valley was named after the company that owned the first well to discover crude oil in the area. Royalties was an oil boom town and was known at one time as "Little Chicago," in reference to the wild parties and all-night poker games. But by 1970, the party was over, and the rowdy nature of the community was only a memory.

RUMSEY This village was named after Reginald Arthur Rumsey, chief inspector and assistant general manager of the Canadian Bank of Commerce. The bank provided financing for the Canadian Northern Railway. Rumsey is east of Trochu and only 12 km northwest of Rowley.

R

RYCROFT Pop. 667. This village was formerly known as Spirit River but was renamed for R.H. Roycroft, a justice of the peace and early settler. Later the spelling on the name was changed to Rycroft. This community is near Spirit River.

RYLEY Pop. 465. This village was named for George Urquhart Ryley. He was a Dominion Land Survey surveyor before taking the position of land commissioner for the Grand Trunk Pacific Railway. Ryley is about 19 km southeast of Tofield.

S

SADDLE MOUNTAIN (2433 m) This is a descriptive name for this saddle-shaped mountain. Saddle Mountain is about 55 km northwest of Banff.

SAGE MOUNTAIN (2368 m) The exact origin of the name for this mountain is uncertain, but it is likely named after the sagebrush in the vicinity. Sage Mountain is about 25 km northwest of Waterton Park.

ST. ALBERT Pop. 56,318. Bishop Alexandre Taché named this place after the patron saint of Father Lacombe. Lacombe was a well-known Oblate of Mary Immaculate missionary. Father Lacombe and Bishop Taché chose this site as a new mission in 1861. St. Albert was incorporated as a city in 1976 and is on the northwest boundary of Edmonton.

MORE ABOUT FATHER LACOMBE...*Born in 1827 at St. Sulphie, Québec, and ordained in 1849, Father Lacombe played an important role in Alberta's history. He participated in nearly every major event of the emerging territory. He set up missions across the province, successfully mediated a dispute between the expanding Canadian Pacific Railway and Chief Crowfoot, and in what was perhaps his hardest challenge, helped prepare Prairie Natives for the disappearance of the buffalo and the loss of the prairies to white settlers. The trust he built with Native leaders was almost legendary. It is said his intervention during a rebellion by the Blackfoot Confederacy prevented the killing of many white settlers on the prairies. His mission-field was large and stretched from Lake Athabasca to the Canada–U.S. border. Father Lacombe covered it without fail for 60 years, ministering to Blackfoot, Cree,*

S

Assiniboine and Métis. Before his death in 1916 at Midnapore, Father Lacombe published a Cree dictionary, Dictionnaire de la langue des Cris.

ST. EDOUARD This hamlet near St. Paul was named after the first name of two pioneers in the area, Edouard Coté and Edouard Labrie.

ST. ELOI MOUNTAIN (2504 m) This mountain was named after a village in Belgium where Canadian troops fought during World War I. St. Eloi Mountain is located about 42 km southwest of Pincher Creek.

ST. JULIEN MOUNTAIN (3091 m) This mountain gets its name from a village in Belgium where Canadian troops fought during World War I. St. Julien Mountain is about 125 km northwest of Banff.

ST. LINA This hamlet was named after Alina Mageau, the wife of a postmaster. St. Lina is 35 km north-northwest of St. Paul.

ST. MICHAEL This hamlet near Lamont was named after the Christian archangel St. Michael.

ST. NICHOLAS PEAK (2970 m) A.O. Wheeler named the peak for a unique formation on its side that he said resembled St. Nicholas (or Santa Claus). St. Nicholas Peak is about 85 km northwest of Banff.

ST. PAUL In 1865, Father Lacombe established the mission of St. Paul des Cris, at the site of today's Brosseau. In 1870, the Catholic settlement project, which intended to teach Cree how to farm, was closed when Lacombe was sent to Québec and France to raise funds for the building of residential schools in western Canada. About 30 years later, Father Therien established St. Paul des Métis, a farm settlement for Métis. Within a few years, its land was opened to European immigrants, and many Ukrainians settled there. Eventually this settlement became the town of St. Paul. Although it is believed the town gets few visitors from outer space, St. Paul maintains the world's only UFO landing pad, a raised platform along a main road in the community. St. Paul is located 115 km northeast of Edmonton. (see Therien)

ST. PIRAN MOUNTAIN (2649 m) This mountain was named after a community in Cornwall, England. St. Piran was the former home of W.J. Astely, a manager of the Lake Louise Chalet. St. Piran is about 60 km northwest of Banff.

SAMSON PEAK (3081 m) Mary Schäffer named this mountain peak near beautiful Maligne Lake in 1911 after Stoney Chief Samson Beaver. Three years earlier, Samson Beaver had drawn a map to guide Mary Schäffer and Molly Adams to Maligne Lake, which Schäffer described as a "mythical lake spoken of by the Indians of Morley." Schäffer and Molly Adams travelled to the lake that year, becoming the first white women to see the lake. Samson Peak is located about 44 km southeast of Jasper. (see Maligne Lake)

SANDY LAKE One of the earliest documented cases of this place name in use was Sir James Hector of the Palliser Expedition referring to "Sandy Lakes" on the trail between Fort Edmonton and Fort Assiniboine in 1859. Sandy Lake is about 44 km northwest of Edmonton.

SANGUDO Pop. 398. There are a couple possible sources for the name of this village near Mayerthorpe. The name may have come from the blending of the slightly misspelled names of two U.S. towns, Santa and Guso (or Guda); or, perhaps, the name was formed by taking the first letter of the names of the original settlers and other relevant words:

S

S for Suttons,

A for Albers,

N for Nanton (where Mrs. Albers formerly lived),

G for Gaskell,

U (for being united in the name of the community),

D for Deep Creek* and

O for Orangeville, the name of the local school district.

*Deep Creek had been chosen to be the area's name, but the idea was dropped because the name was already in use elsewhere.

SANSON PEAK (2256 m) This mountain peak was named after Norman Sanson. He was the official meteorologist at Banff for a number of years. Sanson Peak is near Banff.

SAURIAN MOUNTAIN (3016 m) This mountain was named for its resemblance to the back of a Sauria, a prehistoric lizard. Saurian Mountain is about 119 km northwest of Jasper.

SAWTOOTH MOUNTAIN (2933 m) This mountain about 80 km southeast of Jasper has a descriptive name.

SCANDIA Perhaps this hamlet was named for the large number of settlers from Scandinavia (Scandia), or perhaps the community was named after Scandia, Minnesota, which also had many settlers of Scandinavian descent. Scandia is about 83 km northeast of Lethbridge.

SCAPA This hamlet near Hanna took its name from an Orkney Islands British naval base used in both world wars. In 1919, Germany surrendered its navy at the naval base.

SCARPE MOUNTAIN (2591 m) This mountain was named after a French battlefield where Canadian troops fought in World War I. Scarpe Mountain is 40 km northwest of Waterton Lakes National Park.

S

SCHULER This hamlet was named after postmaster Norman B. Schuler. The community is about 55 km northeast of Medicine Hat.

SCOTFIELD This hamlet was named after William John Scott, because its first post office was located on land owned by Scott. Scotfield is approximately 42 km east of Hanna.

SCOTFORD This locality took its name from the last names of the first premiers of Saskatchewan and Alberta: Walter Scott (Saskatchewan) and Alexander Cameron Rutherford (Alberta). Scotford is about 35 km northeast of Edmonton.

SEBA BEACH Pop. 124. It is believed this summer village was named after the Biblical character Seba, one of the sons of Cush. Seba is about 40 km north-northeast of Drayton Valley.

SEDALIA This hamlet was named after a community of the same name in Missouri from which a few of its early settlers hailed. Sedalia is 38 km north-northwest of Oyen.

SEDGEWICK Pop. 937. This town was named in honour of Robert Sedgewick, a deputy minister of Justice and later a judge of the Supreme Court of Canada. Sedgewick is near Hardisty.

SEEBE The name for this hamlet near Canmore is taken from the Cree word *si-pi*, meaning "creek" or "river."

S

SENTINEL MOUNTAIN (2865 m) This descriptive name refers to the isolated position of this mountain. Sentinel Mountain is about 110 km southwest of Rocky Mountain House.

SENTRY MOUNTAIN (2435 m) This isolated mountain near Coleman was first called Sentinel Mountain but was renamed in 1915 to avoid confusion.

SEVEN PERSONS Pop. 135. This hamlet near Medicine Hat was named after a nearby creek. There are different stories of how Seven Persons Creek received its name. One account tells of a Blood war party led by Chief Calf-Shirt that battled a band of Cree near a creek. Seven Cree were killed and their medicine pipes taken. This site became known as *ki-tsuki-s-tapi*, meaning "seven persons." Another account has it that a railway construction crew discovered seven unmarked graves in the area.

SEVEN SISTERS MOUNTAIN (2591 m) This name refers to the mountain's seven jagged peaks. Seven Sisters Mountain is near Coleman.

SEXSMITH Pop. 1578. This town was named after David Sexsmith, an early resident of the area. The community was originally called Bennville. Sexsmith is near Grande Prairie.

SHAUGHNESSY This hamlet near Lethbridge was named in honour of Thomas George, Lord Shaughnessy. Lord Shaughnessy was president of the Canadian Pacific Railway from 1898 to 1918. He was also president of the Cadillac Coal Company, which operated a coalmine at this hamlet.

SHEERNESS This hamlet was likely named after a seaport in Kent, England. Sheerness is approximately 71 km east of Drumheller.

S

SHEOL MOUNTAIN (2776 m) This mountain took its name from the gloomy and dreary appearance of the valley at its base. The Hebrew *Sheol* is the underworld of the dead. Sheol Mountain is about 50 km west-northwest of Banff.

SHEPARD Pop. 125. This hamlet on the outskirts of Calgary took its name from Shepard of Shepard and Langdon, railway contractors. (see Langdon)

SHERWOOD PARK Pop. 55,063. The name for this community near Edmonton was part of a promotional real-estate marketing plan that drew on associations with England's mythical Robin Hood of Sherwood Forest. At first, this subdivision in the County of Strathcona was known as Campbelltown after its founder John Hook Campbell. Despite its large population, Sherwood Park is only a hamlet, making it one of the largest hamlets in the world. If it was incorporated as a city, it would be the seventh largest city in Alberta.

SHOULDICE This hamlet took its name from James Shouldice, the owner of the land on which the community was built. Shouldice is about 78 km southeast of Calgary.

SIBBALD There are different stories of how this hamlet received its name. Perhaps it was named after John Sibbald, a railway engineer, or possibly after Frank Sibbald, an early rancher in the area. Sibbald is about 177 km east of Drumheller.

SIFFLEUR MOUNTAIN (3129 m) This mountain was so named for the many siffleur, also known as whistling marmots, found nearby. Siffleur Mountain is about 100 km northwest of Banff.

SIGNAL MOUNTAIN (2255 m) This location was used by forest rangers to spot forest fires. Signal Mountain is near Jasper.

SIKSIKA (BLACKFOOT) INDIAN RESERVE # 146 It is generally accepted that the Siksika and Blackfoot name refers to their moccasins, which were painted black or discoloured by the ashes of prairie fires. The Siksika Reserve is about 75 km southeast of Calgary. (see Kainai)

SILVER BEACH The name for this summer village 40 km west-northwest of Wetaskiwin is apparently descriptive.

S

SILVERHORN MOUNTAIN (2911 m) This mountain's name is descriptive of its snow-covered top. Silverhorn Mountain is about 100 km northwest of Banff.

SIMPSON PASS This pass near Banff was named after Sir George Simpson in the early 1800s. He was governor of the Hudson's Bay Company for 40 years. He travelled through this pass in 1841, when he went around the world.

SIRIUS PEAK (2509 m) This mountain peak was named after the brightest star in the sky, Sirius. Sirius Peak, part of the Starlight Range, is about 72 km northwest of Jasper.

SKIFF This hamlet took its name from a small boat or skiff. It is so named, according to some local residents, because of its nearness to a slough that people trying to get to the community crossed by boat. The maritime naming does not stop there. Many of the hamlet's streets and avenues take names from boat parts: Bow Avenue, Stern Avenue, Rudder Street and Tiller Street. Skiff is about 43 nautical miles or 80 km southeast of Lethbridge.

SKOKI MOUNTAIN (2667 m) This mountain took its name from the Native word *skoki*, meaning "marsh" or "swamp." Skoki Mountain is approximately 50 km northwest of Banff.

S

SLAVE LAKE Pop. 6553. This town was named after the nearby Lesser Slave Lake. The community was previously known as Sawridge. Slave Lake is about 190 km southeast of Peace River.

SLIDE MOUNTAIN (2393 m) The name of this mountain commemorates a large rock slide on the western side of the mountain. Slide Mountain is about 38 km south-southwest of Hinton.

SMITH Pop. 264. This hamlet was named after W. Rathbone Smith, a former executive of the Edmonton, Dunvegan and British Columbia Railway. Smith is about 70 km northwest of Athabasca.

SMOKY LAKE Pop. 1087. This town took its name from the nearby lake. The name is a translation of the lake's Cree name *kaskapatau sakahigan*. Folklore has it that this name refers to smoke-like vapour that occasionally rises from the lake, clouding the view to the opposite shore. Smoky Lake is about 88 km northeast of Edmonton.

MORE ABOUT SMOKY LAKE...*About 10 km south of Smoky Lake is the Victoria Settlement. It is a provincial historic site preserving the old Victoria Methodist Mission and a Hudson's Bay Company fur-trading post. The Hudson's Bay clerk's quarters, built in 1864, is the oldest building in Alberta on its original site.*

SMOKY RIVER The Smoky River rises on the eastern slopes of the Rockies in Jasper National Park and flows into the Peace River at the town of Peace River. (see Little Smoky, Swoda Mountain and Watino)

SNAKE INDIAN MOUNTAIN (2929 m) This mountain was named after a small tribe of Natives known as the Snakes. In the early 1800s, some Assiniboine people killed some members of the Snakes tribe during a peace feast. Both parties were to be unarmed at the feast, but the Assiniboine secretly carried in weapons and massacred the others. Snake Indian Mountain is located about 74 km northwest of Jasper.

SNARING MOUNTAIN (2931 m) This mountain was named after a small group of Natives known as the Snare Indians. They gained the name because of the method they used to kill game, with snares made of hide. Snaring Mountain is near Jasper.

S

SNOW DOME MOUNTAIN (3456 m) This mountain was named for its snow-covered dome. Snow Dome Mountain is located about 90 km southeast of Jasper.

SOFA MOUNTAIN (2520 m) This descriptive name refers to a formation on the mountain that resembles a big chesterfield. Sofa Mountain is about 50 km south-southeast of Pincher Creek.

SOLITAIRE MOUNTAIN (3270 m) This descriptive name refers to the isolated position of the mountain. Solitaire Mountain is about 110 km northwest of Banff.

SOUTH SASKATCHEWAN RIVER This river is the southern branch of the 1939-km-long Saskatchewan River. The South Saskatchewan River starts about 85 km east of Lethbridge, where the Oldman River joins the Bow River to form the South Saskatchewan River. The South Saskatchewan River crosses southeastern Alberta, and in Saskatchewan, it is joined by the North Saskatchewan River. Its waters cross several lakes in Saskatchewan and Manitoba before the Nelson River carries them to Hudson Bay. It is one of the great rivers of the prairies. It took its name from the Cree *kis-is-ska-tche-wan*, meaning "swift current."

SPEDDEN There are different stories for how this hamlet was named. It may have been named after R. Speddin, an English sailor who took his yacht to the Arctic to search for the lost Franklin expedition. Or, perhaps the community was named in honour of a Mr. Speddin, who died nearby while working with a survey crew. Spedden is about 33 km west-northwest of St. Paul.

SPHINX MOUNTAIN (2460 m) This descriptive name refers to the mountain's sphinx-like appearance when viewed from the northeast. Sphinx Mountain is approximately 42 km northeast of Jasper.

SPIRIT RIVER Pop. 1112. This town took its name from the nearby Spirit River. The river's name is a translation of its Cree place name *chepi-sipi*, meaning "ghost river." Spirit River is about 65 km north of Grande Prairie.

SPRAY MOUNTAINS The mountains of this range take their name from the spray that comes off the nearby waterfalls in the Bow River. Spray Mountains are 90 km southwest of Calgary. Burstall Mountain is in the Spray Mountains range.

SPRING COULEE This hamlet took its name from a nearby coulee that has many springs. Spring Coulee is about 45 km southwest of Lethbridge.

SPRUCE GROVE Pop. 18,405. Before settlers arrived, there were many spruce trees in the area. Most of the trees have since been logged. The city of Spruce Grove is west of Edmonton.

SPRUCEVIEW Pop. 135. This hamlet took its name from the abundance of spruce in the area. Spruceview is about 25 km northwest of Innisfail.

SPURFIELD The name of this hamlet is a combination of "spur," from the short railway line that served a local lumber company, and Mr. Field, the name of the company manager. Spurfield is east-southeast of Slave Lake.

STAIRWAY PEAK (2999 m) This mountain was named for formations on its side that resemble a stairway. Stairway Peak is about 100 km northwest of Banff.

STANDARD Pop. 366. Perhaps the name for this village, originally a Danish community, refers to the flag of Denmark, which is the oldest of the European Standards (national flags). Standard is located 43 km southwest of Drumheller.

S

STANDOFF This hamlet, where the Waterton River flows into the Belly River, was named after Fort Stand Off, a fort built by U.S. whiskey traders in the early 1870s. The fort was named Stand Off because the whiskey traders had escaped a pursuing U.S. marshal by entering Canada, creating a stand-off, or deadlock, with the marshal. After NWMP constables closed down the whiskey fort, the NWMP built a post nearby with the same name. Standoff is about 43 km southwest of Lethbridge.

STANMORE This hamlet was named after a village in Middlesex, England. Stanmore is near Hanna.

STAR The origin of the name for this hamlet near Lamont is not certain, but it was likely part of a promotion to attract settlers. It has also been known as Edna and Beaver Creek.

STARLIGHT RANGE Three mountains in this range, Arcturus Peak, Sirius Peak and Vega Peak, are named after stars. Starlight Range is about 75 km northwest of Jasper. (see Quoin)

STAVELY Pop. 513. This town took its name from Alexander Staveley Hill, Q.C. Hill was a British MP and the founder and owner of the Oxley Ranching Company. This town was named Oxley, before its name was changed to Stavely, with the second "e" being dropped from the name. The town is about 78 km northwest of Lethbridge.

STETTLER Pop. 5220. This town was named after Carl Stettler, an early homesteader in the area. Stettler was born in Berne, Switzerland and immigrated to the United States. In 1903, he moved to Alberta and started a homestead that became the centre of a German-Swiss community. A post office was opened on Stettler's land. With the arrival of the Canadian Pacific Railway nearby, the post office was moved to the present townsite. Stettler is about 74 km east of Red Deer.

S

STEWART CANYON This canyon was named in the late 1800s after George A. Stewart. He was with the Dominion Lands Survey and later became superintendent of Banff National Park. Stewart Canyon is near Banff.

STIRLING Pop. 874. This village was named after John A. Stirling, managing director of the Trusts, Executors and Securities Corporation. The company, based in London, England, had major holdings in the Alberta Railway and Coal Company. Stirling is about 30 km southeast of Lethbridge.

STONEY SQUAW MOUNTAIN (1868 m) According to legend, this mountain was named after an Assiniboine (Stoney) woman who took care of her ailing husband in a lodge at its foot. Stoney Squaw Mountain is near Banff.

STONY PLAIN Pop. 8274. It is generally accepted this town got its name because its location was well used as a camping area by Stoney Natives. However, the name may stem from Dr. James Hector, geologist of the Palliser Expedition, who noted that the "area well deserves its name for being covered with boulders, which are rather rare in general in this district." Stony Plain is about 30 km west of Edmonton.

MORE ABOUT STONY PLAIN... *Stony Plain is home to the Multicultural Heritage Centre. The centre, a provincial historic site, houses a wide range of past and present culture of the region. In the basement of this "living museum" is the famous Homesteader's Kitchen, which serves pioneer-style meals at reasonable prices. The nearby Oppertshauser House is Alberta's oldest rural public art gallery and is still active.*

S

STRATHCONA COUNTY Pop. 80,232. Strathcona County was formed in 1962 from the old Municipal District of Strathcona, which had been named after the nearby city of Strathcona. (The city of Strathcona amalgamated with the city of Edmonton in 1912.) Prior to 1976, the county office was located in "Old Strathcona" in south Edmonton. In 1976, the office was moved to Sherwood Park, the county's largest population centre. Strathcona was named after Lord Strathcona (Sir Donald Smith), who played an important role in the Canadian Pacific Railway. He had the honour of driving the "last spike" at Craigellachie, finishing construction of the CPR transcontinental line in 1885. Strathcona County borders Edmonton to the east.

STRATHMORE Pop. 6794. This town was named after Claude Bowes-Lyon, 13th Earl of Strathmore. Strathmore is located 45 km east of Calgary.

STREAMSTOWN This hamlet near Lloydminster took its name from a town in Westmeath, Ireland.

STORM MOUNTAIN (3095 m) This mountain located about 47 km west of Turner Valley was named after nearby Storm Creek. Storm Creek got its name when a heavy rainfall hit George Mercer Dawson while he was camping there in 1884. G.M. Dawson (1849–1901) was the namesake of Dawson City, Yukon, and was prominent in the Geological Survey of Canada from 1875 to 1901.

STORM MOUNTAIN (3100 m) This mountain was named by G.M. Dawson in 1884 after the large number of storm clouds on its summit. Storm Mountain is about 30 km west-northwest of Banff.

STROME Pop. 269. There are different versions of how this village southeast of Camrose received its name. Perhaps it was named after Stromeferry, in Ross and Cromarty, Scotland. Another theory is that it was named after a Swedish family living in the area. Strome was previously called Knollton, after Mac Knoll, its first postmaster. The post office opened here in 1906.

STURGEON RIVER This river took its name from the large number of sturgeon fish caught in its waters. The Cree name for the river is *mi-koo-oo-pow*, meaning "red willow." The river is located about 33 km from Edmonton, carrying water from Lac Ste. Anne to the North Saskatchewan River at Fort Saskatchewan. (see Namao)

STURGEON VALLEY This hamlet took its name from the nearby Sturgeon River. Sturgeon Valley is near Edmonton.

STUTFIELD PEAK (3396 m) This mountain was named after Hugh E. Stutfield. He was a member of the Alpine Club of London and the co-author of *Climbs and Explorations in the Canadian Rockies* (1903). Stutfield Peak is about 85 km southeast of Jasper.

SUFFIELD Pop. 201. This hamlet near Medicine Hat was named after Charles Harbord, Fifth Baron Suffield. Suffield is the location of a large military training base and a biological research facility.

SULPHUR MOUNTAIN (2451 m) This mountain near Banff took its name from the sulphur hot springs at its base.

SUNDANCE BEACH Pop. 35. The name of this summer village commemorates Native Sun Dances, week-long cultural ceremonies in which bands and tribes socialized and dancers underwent self-torture for days to garner lifelong prestige. Sundance Beach is about 50 km west-northwest of Wetaskiwin.

SUNDIAL MOUNTAIN (3182 m) This descriptive name is derived from a sundial-shaped feature on the mountain. Sundial Mountain is about 80 km southeast of Jasper.

SUNDRE Pop. 2190. This town was named by its first postmaster and an early settler, N.T. Hagan. He named his new

S

home after Sundre, Norway. Sundre is located 77 km southwest of Red Deer.

SUNNYBROOK This hamlet on the banks of a creek, or brook, has a descriptive name. It is about 27 km west-southwest of Calmar.

SUNNYNOOK Residents in this area put this name forward to the Canadian National Railway, who made it official. The name is meant to be evocative of Alberta's long sunny summer days. Sunnynook is about 75 km east-southeast of Drumheller.

SUNNYSLOPE This hamlet near Three Hills was named by Peter Giesbrecht, its first postmaster. He chose a descriptive name that refers to the sunny vistas in the area.

SUNSET PEAK (3265 m) This mountain likely took its name from a sun setting on its peak. It was named in 1929 by Richard W. Cautley of the Alberta–BC Inter-Provincial Boundary Commission. Sunset Peak is located about 89 km northwest of Jasper. (see Mount Cautley)

SUNWAPTA PEAK (3265 m) This peak was named after the nearby Sunwapta River, which flows into the Athabasca River south of Jasper. *Sunwapta* is a Stoney term meaning "turbulent river." Sunwapta Peak is about 75 km south-southeast of Jasper.

SURVEY PEAK (2334 m) J.N. Collie and H.E. Stutfield (of Stutfield Peak fame) climbed this mountain in 1898. They made the ascent to conduct a plane table survey of the vicinity. Survey Peak is approximately 120 km northwest of Banff.

SWALWELL Pop. 76. This hamlet was named after an official of the Grand Trunk Pacific Railway, Mr. Swalwell. Previously this community was known as Rawdonville. Swalwell is near Three Hills.

SWAN HILLS Pop. 2030. This town took its name from the nearby Swan Hills. These hills, according to Native legend, are the home of thunderbirds—large birds that cause the sound of thunder by flapping their wings. As the legend goes, it is unwise to enter the hills where the birds live. Happily, the legends say the birds have never harmed people, and they have never even been seen. The town of Swan Hills, about 75 km southwest of Slave Lake, was established in 1959 to service the oilfield work in the area.

SWODA MOUNTAIN (3003 m) This mountain took its name from the Stoney name for the nearby Smoky River. Swoda Mountain is about 82 km northwest of Jasper.

SYLVAN LAKE Pop. 5178. This resort town near Red Deer took its name from the nearby lake. The lake had previously been known as Snake Lake, Methy Lake and Swan Lake, before taking its current name prior to 1900. *Sylvan*, Latin for "wood," can be used to describe something relating to woodlands. Thus, the name is evocative of a beautiful, peaceful place.

SYNCLINE MOUNTAIN (2441 m) This mountain took its name from the syncline (rock folded into a trough) feature in the Devonian rocks on the mountain's ridge. Syncline Mountain is about 29 km northwest of Blairmore.

S

T

TABER Pop. 7331. There are different versions of how this town was named. Perhaps the name came from the first part of the word Tabernacle, in recognition of the large number of Mormon settlers in the area. Or, the town may have been named after Mount Tabor (near the Sea of Galilee). It is also possible that Taber was named after a CPR official or after U.S. Senator Tabor. Taber is about 48 km east of Lethbridge.

TABLE MOUNTAIN (2232 m) This mountain located near Pincher Creek is shaped like a table.

TAIL CREEK This creek located near Stettler was named for its long, narrow shape that resembles a tail.

MORE ABOUT TAIL CREEK… *Tail Creek Town, near Tail Creek, was used in the 1870s by Métis and other Natives for organized buffalo hunts. At one time, the community was larger than Edmonton, with about 400 log cabins. But in 1877, the buffalo disappeared from the area and with them went the buffalo hunters, who had used Tail Creek as a meeting and resting place. A fire destroyed most of the buildings, and what remained was taken to Stettler, where a monument recounts the memory of the once-busy town.*

TALLON PEAK (1829 m) There are different versions of how this mountain peak near Bellevue was named. Perhaps it was named after L. Tallon, who was involved in surveys of the Rockies, or perhaps the shape of this peak resembles an eagle's talon.

TANGENT This hamlet was so named because it was the start of a 50-km-long tangent, or straight length, of railway track along the Edmonton, Dunvegan and British Columbia Railway (which later became a branch of the Canadian National Railway). Tangent is near Falher.

TATEI RIDGE The name of this ridge 73 km west-northwest of Jasper is the Stoney term for "wind."

TAWATINAW This hamlet was named after the nearby Tawatinaw River. *Tawatinaw* is Cree for "river which divides the hills." Tawatinaw is near Westlock.

TELFORDVILLE This hamlet was named after Robert T. Telford, an early settler in the area. Telford served in the North-West Mounted Police in the late 1800s and, from 1905 to 1913, was a Liberal member of the Alberta Legislature, representing the Leduc area. Telfordville is about 52 km southwest of Edmonton.

TENT MOUNTAIN (2197 m) This mountain located near Coleman is shaped like a tent.

TERMINAL MOUNTAIN (2835 m) This mountain was named for its location at the end of a ridge. Terminal Mountain is near Jasper.

TERRACE MOUNTAIN (2917 m) This mountain 105 km southeast of Jasper took its name from its terrace-like shape.

TERRAPIN MOUNTAIN (2926 m) This mountain was named for its resemblance to a turtle. Mount Terrapin is about 105 km west of Calgary.

T

THERIEN This hamlet was named in honour of Rev. J. Adéodat Therien of the Oblates of Mary Immaculate. Father Therien was the first director of nearby St. Paul des Métis, which became the town of St. Paul.

THISTLE MOUNTAIN (2860 m) This mountain took its name from nearby Thistle Creek, which was named after the thistle that grows nearby. Thistle Mountain is located east-southeast of Jasper.

THORHILD Pop. 486. It is believed the name of this village refers to Thor, the god of thunder in Norse mythology. Its first postmaster, Glen Jardy, chose the name Thor's Hill, because of the frequent lighting strikes at a nearby hill. The post office opened here in 1914. Thorhild is 92 km northeast of Edmonton.

THORSBY Pop. 725. This village took its name from Thor, the god of thunder in Norse mythology, and *by*, the Norse word for "village." Thorsby is about 49 km southwest of Edmonton.

THREE HILLS Pop. 3375. This town was named after three nearby hills. Three Hills is about 75 km south-southeast of Red Deer.

THREE SISTERS, THE (2829 m on average) The three mountain peaks on this ridge near Canmore are named for their resemblance to one another.

THREEPOINT MOUNTAIN (2595 m) This mountain 39 km west of Turner Valley was named for its three peaks.

THRONE MOUNTAIN (3120 m) This mountain was named for its shape, which resembles a big chair. Throne Mountain is about 33 km north-northwest of Jasper.

TILLEY Pop. 368. Perhaps this village was named after one of Canada's Fathers of Confederation, Sir Samuel Leonard Tilley. Tilley served as a cabinet minister and premier in the New Brunswick Legislature and then in the federal government as minister of Customs and of Finance. There is also an account that this village was named after Samuel Tilley's brother, Sir Malcolm Tilley, who was a director of the Canadian Pacific Railway. Tilley is about 83 km northwest of Medicine Hat.

TILTED MOUNTAIN (2591 m) This mountain was named after its tilting rocks. Tilted Mountain is located about 45 km northwest of Banff.

TITKANA PEAK (2804 m) The name for this mountain comes from the Stoney word for "bird." Titkana Peak is 74 km west-northwest of Jasper.

TOFIELD Pop. 1726. This town was named after Dr. J.H. Tofield, an early settler in the district. Dr. Tofield obtained two degrees from Oxford, one in medicine and the other in engineering. Dr. Tofield decided to practise medicine and served as an army doctor in India. He later came to Alberta where he practised medicine among the Cree and white settlers. Tofield is about 57 km east-southeast of Edmonton.

MORE ABOUT TOFIELD...*Every year, Tofield hosts the Beaverhill Lake Snow Goose Festival on the third weekend of April. It is an opportunity to see thousands of migrating Snow geese, Canada geese, shorebirds, cranes and swans return to nearby Beaverhill Lake. The large, shallow lake provides a place for migrating birds to rest and feed. Each year, some 7000 people visit Beaverhill Lake and Tofield during the two-day festival.*

TOMAHAWK Pop. 92. This hamlet took its name from Tomahawk, Wisconsin. It was so named by the first settler in the area, Lewis Shaw. Tomahawk is near Drayton Valley.

TOMBSTONE MOUNTAIN (3035 m) The name describes this mountain about 50 km west of Turner Valley. The mountain has a large number of slabs at its summit.

TORNADO MOUNTAIN (3236 m) This mountain is so named because of the frequency of storms around its summit. Tornado Mountain is about 40 km northwest of Coleman.

T

TORY MOUNTAIN (2831 m) This mountain was named after Dr. Henry Marshall Tory. Tory was the first president of the University of Alberta and had a long, distinguished career in academia. He served as the first chairman of the National Research Council and on several royal commissions.

MORE ABOUT DR. TORY... *In 1908 Dr. Henry Marshall Tory founded the University of Alberta in Strathcona (later a part of Edmonton). He was also the principal founder of the University of British Columbia, Carleton University, the Alberta Research Council and the National Research Council Laboratories. Dr. Tory trained for the ministry, but after a couple of years preaching in Montréal, he accepted a position to lecture in mathematics at McGill. He obtained a Doctorate of Science from McGill and became a roving ambassador for the university. Settling in Alberta, Dr. Tory took on the job of establishing the University of Alberta. He was its president for 20 years, leaving his mark on the university as a centre for scientific research and adult education. Part of his innovative approach for "taking the university to the people" was a travelling rural library and the use of radio. In 1928, Dr. Tory left the province to establish Carleton University and to set up the National Research Council (NRC) in Ottawa. Dr. Tory considered the establishment of the NRC his largest contribution to education and science in Canada.*

T

TOTEM TOWER (3105 m) This mountain was named after nearby Totem Creek. The origin of the creek's name is not certain. Totem Tower is about 105 km west of Calgary.

TOWER OF BABEL (2310 m) This mountain is so named because of its likeness to the Tower of Babel in The Bible. Tower of Babel is located about 45 km west-northwest of Banff.

TOWERS, THE (2846 m) This mountain 105 km west of Calgary was named for its many turret-like peaks.

TRAPPER PEAK (2984 m) This mountain was named after Bill Peyto. He was a well-known Rocky Mountain guide and trapper. Trapper Peak is about 90 km northwest of Banff. (see Peyto Peak)

TRIAD PEAK (3058 m) This name is descriptive of this peak 90 km southeast of Jasper.

TRIDENT RANGE This range took its name from its three-pronged shape. Trident Range is near Jasper.

TROCHU Pop. 958. This town about 62 km south-southwest of Red Deer was named after Colonel Armand Trochu. Trochu, with a few other former French cavalry officers, established the St. Ann Ranch Trading Company in the early 1900s. Many of the officers returned to France with the outbreak of World War I. The St. Ann Ranch Museum contains more than 1000 photographs and other materials depicting life at the ranch. The community was first known as Trochu Valley and later became Trochu.

TUNNEL MOUNTAIN (1692 m) A tunnel was planned for this mountain during construction of the Canadian Pacific Railway transcontinental line, but an engineer of the project found a different route, and the tunnel was not built. The name, however, remained. Tunnel Mountain is near Banff.

TURIN This hamlet was named after a Percheron stallion owned by a group of area farmers. (Percheron horses originate from the Perche region of France). Turin is about 35 km northeast of Lethbridge.

TURNER VALLEY Pop. 1575. This town was named after the valley in which it is located. The valley was named after

T

Robert and James Turner. Formerly of Edinburgh, Scotland, the Turners were early settlers in the area and were the first to observe signs of oil in the district. The first major discovery of oil took place in 1914, and until the Leduc oilfield was discovered in 1947, Turner Valley was the big producer of oil in Canada. This community is about 40 km southwest of Calgary.

MORE ABOUT TURNER VALLEY... *One man set in motion the "Fantastic Calgary Oil Boom" of 1914 in Turner Valley. He was Archibald Wayne Dingman. One of nine children from a United Empire Loyalist family, Archibald grew up in Ontario. In the 1880s, he worked in the oilfields of Pennsylvania. After gaining experience in the oil business, he returned to Canada, where, instead of following his ambition to find oil in his home country, he became involved in a soap company. Dingman had a talent for business and did well selling soap, but the factory burned to the ground in 1900. A couple of years after the loss of his business, Dingman decided to move west and again take up his interest of searching for oil. In 1905, he set up the Calgary Gas Company and drilled a well on the Sarcee Reserve. The well proved unsuccessful. Dingman had better success on his second try with the Walker Well, which provided enough gas to heat houses and light streets in parts of Calgary. Encouraged by this success, Dingman established the Calgary Petroleum Products Company in 1912. It was this company that drilled the history-making Dingman No. 1 well in Turner Valley, discovering Alberta's first major gas and oil field. After World War II, the oil play shifted north to the Leduc area.*

T

TURTLE MOUNTAIN (2204 m) The name is descriptive of this mountain, which resembles the shape of a turtle. The village of Frank is located at the foot of this mountain about 220 km west of Calgary. A part of Frank was destroyed by Turtle Mountain's massive 1903 rock slide. (see Frank)

TWEEDIE This locality near Lac La Biche was named after Alberta politician Thomas Mitchell March Tweedie (1871–1944). Tweedie served as a Conservative MLA and MP during the 1910s before being named to the Supreme Court of Alberta. In 1944, he was named chief justice of the Supreme Court of Alberta.

TWIN BUTTE The name of this locality refers to two large hills in the area. Twin Butte is about 90 km southwest of Lethbridge.

TWIN PEAKS (height unknown) This is a descriptive name for this mountain. Twin Peaks is located 70 km southwest of Turner Valley.

TWINS,THE This mountain was named The Twins, because it has two peaks, North Twin (3684 m) and South Twin (3559 m). The Twins, 85 km southeast of Jasper, was named by H.E. Stutfield (of Stutfield Peak fame) in 1898.

TWINTREE MOUNTAIN (2544 m) This mountain was named after two spruce trees on nearby lake islets. Twin-tree Mountain is about 92 km west-northwest of Jasper.

TWO HILLS Pop. 1040. This town took its name from two prominent hills southwest of the community. The community was previously known as Poserville. Two Hills is about 115 km northeast of Edmonton.

T

U

UNCAS This locality was named after a town in Oklahoma. Uncas is near Edmonton.

UPRIGHT MOUNTAIN (2944 m) This mountain took its name from the unique orientation of its rock strata. The mountain's rocks are oriented almost vertically. Upright Mountain is located about 63 km west-northwest of Jasper.

USONA This locality took the name of a community in California. Usona has the first letters of the words "United States of North America." Usona is 20 km southwest of Wetaskiwin.

UTOPIA MOUNTAIN (2602 m) This mountain does not take its name from lofty political ideals. Utopia Mountain was so named by surveyors who found the mountain free from the flies they had found in profusion elsewhere. Utopia Mountain is located 40 km southwest of Hinton.

V

VALAD PEAK (3150 m) This mountain was named after a Métis guide who accompanied CPR surveyor Henry A.F. MacLeod to Maligne Lake in 1875. Valad Peak is located 63 km southwest of Jasper. (see Mount Henry MacLeod)

VALHALLA This locality took its name from Norse mythology. The mythical Valhalla is the home of Viking heroes after they die. The community is about 49 km northwest of Grande Prairie.

VALHALLA CENTRE Pop. 48. This hamlet has the same origin for its name as Valhalla. The centre is about 42 km northwest of Grande Prairie.

VALLEY HEAD MOUNTAIN (2607 m) This mountain took its name from its location at the head of the Brazeau River valley. Valley Head Mountain is about 57 km west of Nordegg.

VALLEY OF THE TEN PEAKS, THE The Valley of the Ten Peaks, about 45 km west-northwest of Banff, was previously known as Desolation Valley. The ten peaks that surround this valley were originally named using Stoney words for the numerals one to ten, but almost all have been renamed. The peaks include Mount Fay, Mount Allen, Mount Tuzo, Deltaform Mountain, Neptuak Mountain and Wenkchema Peak.

VALLEYVIEW Pop. 1944. This is a descriptive name for the community about 100 km east of Grande Prairie. A view of the Red Willow and Sturgeon Creeks can be seen from the town.

VAUXHALL Pop. 1011. This town was named after Vauxhall, a district in London, England. Vauxhall is about 68 km northeast of Lethbridge.

VEGA This locality was named after a piece of equipment familiar to many homesteaders, the Vega cream separator. Vega is about 30 km north of Barrhead.

VEGA PEAK (2491 m) This mountain in the Starlight Range was named after the star of the same name. Vega Peak is about 75 km northwest of Jasper.

VEGREVILLE Pop. 5337. This town was named after Father Valentin Vegreville, an Oblate of Mary Immaculate missionary. He worked as a missionary in western Canada for 50 years. Father Vegreville was also a linguist in the Cree, Montagnais and Assiniboine (Stoney) languages. The first settlers in the 1890s were French farmers from Kansas, but Vegreville later became a Ukrainian settlement. The post office opened in 1895. Vegreville is located about 95 km east of Edmonton.

MORE ABOUT VEGREVILLE... *Vegreville is home to the world's largest pysanka, a traditional Ukrainian decorated Easter egg. Built to commemorate the 1974 centennial celebrations of the Royal Canadian Mounted Police, this giant pysanka is the result of the first computer modelling of an egg. It is 9.4 m tall, 5.5 m wide and 7.8 m long. The egg weighs close to 2300 kg, and a specially designed stand allows it to turn in the wind like a weathervane.*

The various colours and designs of the pysanka symbolize themes that vary from the "good earth" that provided pioneers with a living to the RCMP's role in maintaining law and order in the area.

VENICE This hamlet was named after Venice, Italy. It was so named by O.J. Biollo, its first postmaster and an early settler in the area. Venice is near Lac La Biche.

VERMILION Pop. 4303. This town located on the Vermilion River was named after the river, which has iron-rich deposits along its valley. The iron rusts, turning the water and soil red, giving the river its name. Vermilion River flows into the North Saskatchewan River from the south, while the similarly named Redwater River flows into it from the north. Vermilion is about 56 km west of Lloydminster.

VERMILION LAKES The name of this chain of lakes near Banff refers to the area's iron-rich deposits, which are reddish-brown (or vermilion) in colour.

VERTEX PEAK (2957 m) This mountain was named for its sharp triangular summit. A corner of a triangle is an example of a vertex. Vertex Peak is near Jasper.

VETERAN Pop. 317. This village was named to mark the coronation in 1911 of King George V. Veteran is about 26 km east-southeast of Coronation. The community was previously known as Wheatbelt.

VIKING Pop. 1081. This town was named by Norwegian settlers after their Viking ancestors. Viking is about 70 km east-northeast of Camrose.

MORE ABOUT VIKING... *Near Viking, ribstones that date back 1000 years lie in a farmer's field. The stones display carvings that resemble a bison's rib and held spiritual significance for the Natives in the area, who relied on the bison for food and clothing. By holding ceremonial rites at the ribstones, Natives hoped to improve their chances of successful bison hunting.*

VILLENEUVE Pop. 174. This hamlet near Edmonton was named after Frederick Villeneuve. Villeneuve was a lawyer and represented St. Albert in the North-West Territories Legislative Assembly. The community was formerly known as St. Peter's and St. Pierre.

VILNA Pop. 302. This village took its name from the hometown of Galician immigrants who settled the area. Galicia was a province in the Austro-Hungarian Empire. Vilna is 36 km east of Smoky Lake.

VIMY This hamlet was named after the World War I Battle of Vimy Ridge (April 9–17, 1917) in France. The battle was the first time Canadian soldiers fought as a corps under Canadian command. After careful preparation and with the support of artillery, the Canadians achieved a major victory. They swept the German troops off the long, low ridge and took the strategic position that had linked the German's new Hindenburg Line to their main trench lines near Arras, France. Canadians gained more ground and took more prisoners than any previous British offensive. The success at Vimy Ridge boosted morale and gave Canadians confidence in their fighting abilities. Vimy is near Westlock.

VIMY PEAK (2385 m) Vimy Peak was named after a famous World War I Canadian victory. Vimy Peak is located 50 km south-southeast of Pincher Creek. (see Vimy)

VISTA PEAK (2795 m) This mountain was named after the view seen from this point. Vista Peak is near Banff.

VULCAN Pop. 1677. This town took its name from the Roman god of fire and metalworking. Vulcan is 85 km south-southeast of Calgary.

V

WABAMUN Pop. 645. This village took its name from the lake on which it is situated. *Wabamun*, Cree for "mirror," possibly refers to the stillness of the lake. Wabamun is 65 km west of Edmonton. (see Kapasiwin)

WABASCA/DESMARAIS Pop. 1028. In 1982, Wabasca and nearby Desmarais combined to make one hamlet. *Wabasca* is a Native word meaning "grassy narrows," which possibly refers to the nearby slender neck that connects North Wabasca Lake and South Wabasca Lake. Desmarais was named in honour of Father Alphonse Desmarais, an Oblate missionary. This community is about 90 km northeast of Lesser Slave Lake.

WAINWRIGHT Pop. 5219. This town was named in 1908 after William Wainwright, a senior executive of the Grand Trunk Pacific Railway. The community was formerly known as Denwood. Wainwright is about 75 km southwest of Lloydminster. (see Irma)

WALL OF JERICHO (2910 m) This mountain has a precarious shape and appears to be tumbling down as in the Biblical story of the Walls of Jericho. This mountain is located 55 km northwest of Banff.

WALSH Pop. 74. This hamlet just inside Alberta was named in honour of NWMP Superintendent James Morrow Walsh. Superintendent Walsh set up Fort Walsh in the Cypress Hills, just east of what would be the Alberta–Saskatchewan border, in 1875. Walsh is located about 45 km east of Medicine Hat.

MORE ABOUT JAMES WALSH…*After decisively winning the Battle of Little Big Horn in 1876, Chief Sitting Bull and 5000 followers fled across the unmarked Canada–U.S. border into the Wood Mountains of southern Saskatchewan. With the political landscape in flux in the region, Chief Sitting Bull's arrival was unnerving for Ottawa. Major Walsh of the newly formed North-West Mounted Police was given the job of taking control of the potentially volatile situation. Walsh gained a reputation for firmness in dealing with Sitting Bull. The Sioux chief failed to convince Canadian chiefs to form an alliance to fight the NWMP and the new settlers on the Prairies. With time, Sitting Bull's influence waned among his followers and others. The Sioux chief stayed in Canada for five years before returning to the United States, where he was imprisoned. He was later killed by members of his tribe.*

WANDERING RIVER This hamlet took its name from the nearby river. Wandering River is about 58 km northwest of Lac La Biche.

WANHAM Pop. 167. There are different accounts of how this village about 69 km northeast of Grande Prairie was named. Perhaps its name was derived from a Native word that translates as "warm winds," or perhaps it was named after a community in England.

WAPITI MOUNTAIN (3028 m) This mountain took its name from the nearby Wapiti River. *Wapiti* is a Native word for "elk." Wapiti Mountain is about 65 km northwest of Banff.

WAPUTIK PEAK (2736 m) This peak is located about 65 km northwest of Banff. (see Waputik Range)

WAPUTIK RANGE When this range was named in the late 1800s, it was a favorite place for mountain goats. *Waputik* is the Stoney word for "white goat." Waputik Range is about 65 km northwest of Banff.

WARBURG Pop. 549. This village took its name from an old castle in Sweden. The castle name is Warberg, but this was misspelled in the Alberta name. Warburg is about 50 km southwest of Edmonton.

WARDEN ROCK (2696 m) This is a descriptive name for this mountain, which resembles a warden on guard. Warden Rock is located about 60 km north of Banff.

WARDLOW It is widely believed this hamlet was named after a daughter of J.R. Sutherland, an area rancher. Another account claims it was named by the Canadian National Railway, but it is not known why the CNR picked this name. Wardlow is 115 km northwest of Medicine Hat.

WARNER Pop. 420. This village about 60 km southeast of Lethbridge was named after A.L. Warner, a land agent. The community was previously called Brunton.

WARRIOR MOUNTAIN (2926 m) This mountain was named after a British cruiser that took part in the 1916 Battle of Jutland. Warrior Mountain is located 70 km west-southwest of Turner Valley.

WARSPITE Pop. 75. This village near Smoky Lake took its name from the British cruiser HMS *Warspite*, which took part in the 1916 Battle of Jutland. Mount Warspite is also named after this warship.

WASKATENAU Pop. 237. The name for this village comes from its Cree place name *Waskatenau*, meaning "opening in the banks." The Waskatenau Creek flows through an opening in a nearby ridge on its way to the North Saskatchewan River. Waskatenau, pronounced with a silent "K," is near Smoky Lake.

WASTACH PASS (2544 m) This pass took its name from the Stoney word that means "beautiful." Wastach Pass is located about 55 km northwest of Banff.

WATCHTOWER, THE (2791 m) This mountain was named for its tower-like appearance. The Watchtower is near Jasper.

WATER VALLEY This hamlet may have been given a descriptive name, or it may have been named after a location in Colorado. Water Valley is about 32 km south of Sundre.

WATERHOLE This locality near Fairview was named for a favorite camping and watering site of homesteaders as they journeyed into Peace River country. Waterhole is located on the old Dunvegan-Peace River Trail.

WATERTON LAKES, WATERTON LAKES NATIONAL PARK The Waterton Lakes are four lakes connected by the Waterton River: the Maskinonge Lake and the Lower, Middle and Upper Waterton Lakes. The Waterton Lakes are situated in the main valley of Waterton Lakes National Park. The Waterton River was named after English naturalist Charles Waterton (1782–1865). He was the author of several books, including *Wandering in South America, the North West of the United States and the Antilles in 1812, 1816, 1820 and 1824*. Although his journeys took him far and wide, he never visited Canada. The Waterton Lakes are located about 50 km south of Pincher Creek, right on the Canada–U.S. border.

WATERTON PARK This hamlet sits within Waterton Lakes National Park. Waterton Park is about 50 km south of Pincher Creek. (see Waterton Lakes)

WATINO It is believed the name for this hamlet was taken from a Cree word that translates as "valley." The hamlet was previously known as Smoky, likely after nearby Smoky River. Watino is about 80 km southwest of the town of Peace River.

WEDGE, THE (2652 m) This is a descriptive name for the mountain's wedge-like summit. The Wedge is located about 70 km west of Calgary.

WELLING This hamlet near Lethbridge was named after Horace Welling, an early settler in the area.

WEMBLEY Pop. 1523. The name for this town was chosen at the time of the 1924 British Empire Exposition in Wembley, England. Wembley is near Grande Prairie.

MORE ABOUT WEMBLEY... *One person who put Wembley and the Peace River district on the world agricultural map was Herman Trelle. He won some 135 championships for his crops, which included wheat and oats. Trelle's remarkable ability as a plant breeder started with cross-breeding strains of wheat. By 1920, he was growing his own registered grain. In 1926, he won two major awards; the world wheat championship in Chicago and world honours for his Victory oats. He later won the world wheat championship for three consecutive years. In 1932, Trelle was banned from competition, because he was winning the title too often. When he was allowed back in, in 1936, he again took the title of top world wheat grower. During World War II he served a short time with the Royal Canadian Engineers in Ontario. After being discharged for medical reasons, Trelle did not return to farming. He eventually ended up as a supervisor for a ranching operation in California. He died there after being shot by a ranch hand whom he had fired.*

WENKCHEMNA PEAK (3170 m) This mountain peak is the 10th in the Valley of the Ten Peaks. The Stoney word *wenkchemna* translates as "10." Wenkchemna Peak is located 55 km west-northwest of Banff.

WEST BAPTISTE Pop. 36. This summer village near Athabasca is located on the western shore of Baptiste Lake.

Baptiste Lake took its name from an early settler in the area, Baptiste Majeau.

WESTLOCK Pop. 4817. The area's first settlement, located near the present townsite, was called Edison. In 1912, land for a new townsite was purchased from settlers by the name of Westage and Lockhart. Westlock was formed from these two names. Westlock is about 75 km northwest of Edmonton.

WESTWARD HO The name for this hamlet was suggested by a British army officer and settler, Captain Thomas. He had gotten the name from Charles Kingsley's novel *Westward Ho*. Westward Ho is near Sundre.

WETASKIWIN Pop. 10,959. After a battle between the Cree and Blackfoot in 1867, the two sides came together at this location to end fighting and enter into a treaty. The Cree called it *wi-ta-ski-winik*, meaning "place of peace." The Blackfoot referred to the location as *inuststi-tomo*, meaning "peace hills." The present name is taken from the Cree word. The city is located about 70 km south of Edmonton.

MORE ABOUT WETASKIWIN...*A number of museums are in Wetaskiwin: Alberta Central Railway Museum, Canada's Aviation Hall of Fame, Reynolds-Alberta Museum, Reynolds Aviation Museum, Reynolds Museum, and Wetaskiwin and District Museum. The Reynolds-Alberta Museum, in a league of its own, presents the history of transportation, agricultural machinery and other industries in Alberta. The exhibits display artifacts from the 1890s to the 1950s. A hangar that houses Canada's Aviation Hall of Fame is next to the museum. The Aviation Hall of Fame recognizes those who made a contribution to aviation and contains several vintage aircraft, ranging from a Gypsy Moth biplane to a Beech aircraft.*

WHALEBACK RIDGE This is a descriptive name for this ridge, which resembles the back of a whale. Whaleback Ridge is about 35 km northeast of Blairmore.

WHISTLER MOUNTAIN (height unknown) The origin of this name is uncertain. It is likely this mountain took its name from the many whistling marmots in the area. Whistler Mountain is about 35 km southwest of Pincher Creek.

WHISTLERS, THE (2466 m) This mountain near Jasper took its name from the whistling marmots found in its vicinity.

WHITE MAN MOUNTAIN (2977 m) This mountain about 95 km west-southwest of Calgary is likely named after Father de Smet. (see White Man Pass)

WHITE MAN PASS (2168 m) This pass took its name from its Native place name *shakooap-te-ha-wapta*. It likely refers to the Belgium missionary Father de Smet, who in 1845, crossed the Rocky Mountains using the pass. White Man Pass is about 95 km west-southwest of Calgary. Roche de Smet is also named after him.

WHITECOURT Pop. 8008. This town is a combination of the name of Walter White, the community's first postmaster, and White's hometown of Greencourt. Cree named this location *sak-de-wah*, roughly translated as "where the waters come together." Whitecourt, 158 km northwest of Edmonton, is located where the McLeod River flows into the Athabasca River.

WHITECROW MOUNTAIN (2831 m) This mountain took its name from the white crows in the area. Whitecrow Mountain is located about 37 km southwest of Jasper.

WHITELAW In 1924, this hamlet near Fairview was named after Mr. Whitelaw, a Central Canada Railway employee.

WHITFORD This hamlet east of Andrew took its name from a common last name among the Métis living in the area during the 1890s. The area's Métis Whitford clan descended from an HBC employee of that name, according to 1916 local postmaster Andrew Whitford (the namesake of the nearby village of Andrew). The Cree name for this location was *munawanis*, meaning "where the eggs are gathered." The large Whitford Lake is well used by migrating and nesting birds.

WIDEWATER The name for this hamlet refers to its location on the banks of Lesser Slave Lake where the lake is particularly wide. Widewater is 18 km northwest of Slave Lake.

WILCOX PASS (2347 m) This pass took its name from Walter Dwight Wilcox. It is thought he was the first white man to cross the pass. In the early 1900s, Wilcox authored *The Rockies of Canada*. Wilcox Pass is about 90 km southeast of Jasper. Nearby Mount Wilcox is also named after him.

WILDWOOD This hamlet was named for its bushy surroundings. This hamlet is about 38 km south of Mayerthorpe.

WILLINGDON Pop. 309. This village was named in honour of Governor General Freeman Freeman-Thomas, Viscount Willingdon of Ratton. Viscount Willingdon (1866–1941) served as governor general from 1926 to 1931 and then as viceroy of India. Willingdon is 97 km east-northeast of Edmonton.

WILLMORE WILDERNESS PARK This provincial park of 4568 square kilometres was set up in 1959 and was named after Norman A. Willmore (1909–65). He served in Alberta's Social Credit government as minister of Lands and Forests. This park northwest of Jasper contains mountain peaks, glaciers, alpine meadows and river valleys.

WIMBORNE It is believed this hamlet was named after a community of the same name in Dorset, England. Wimborne is near Trochu.

WINDSOR MOUNTAIN (2544 m) The profile of this mountain bears a likeness to the shape of Windsor Castle in England. Windsor Mountain is about 30 km southwest of Pincher Creek.

WINDFALL This hamlet took its name from the nearby creek of the same name. Windfall Creek may have been named by travellers who encountered many trees knocked down by the wind. Windfall is near Whitecourt.

WINFIELD This hamlet was named after Vernor Winfield Smith (1864–1932). Smith served as a cabinet minister in the provincial UFA government and was also a successful Camrose farmer. Winfield is 47 km southeast of Drayton Valley.

WOKING This hamlet was named after Woking in Surrey, near London. This English place name goes back in history at least as far as 1086 when the *Domesday Book* lists a "Wochinges" and refers to the followers and home of a man named "Wocca." Alberta's Woking is 45 km north of Grande Prairie.

WOOD BUFFALO NATIONAL PARK Wood Buffalo National Park, located about 260 km northwest of Fort McMurray, is Canada's largest national park. It is 44,804 square kilometres in area, 9388 square kilometres of which are in the Northwest Territories. The park took its name from the resident wood buffalo. These bison, as compared to plains bison, live in wooded areas and have darker coats. The park was established in 1922 to protect the world's largest remaining herd of wood buffalo. The park's bison now number about 2500.

WOOLFORD This hamlet was named after Thomas Henry Woolford, a settler in the area. Woolford is about 60 km southwest of Lethbridge.

WORSLEY There are different versions of how this hamlet was named. Perhaps the community was named after

Eric Worsley. Worsley was a former British cavalry officer who lived in the Peace River area. He returned to England with the outbreak of World War I, signed up to fight and was killed in action. Another possible source for the name is the name of a village in England. Worsley is about 65 km northwest of Fairview.

WOSTOK Wostok is located about 76 km northeast of Edmonton. This hamlet took its name from the Russian word *vostok*, meaning "east." It was settled by immigrants from Galicia in the 1890s. Ukrainian emigration promoter Joseph Oleskow led a group of settlers to the end-of-steel at Strathcona (Old Strathcona, Edmonton), then to this area in east-central Alberta. Krakow, 10 km south of Wostok, was settled by immigrants from the same area at about the same time.

WRENTHAM Many people believe this hamlet was named after a village in the county of Suffolk, England. However, some oldtimers claim there is another story. Apparently, many of the homesteaders were poor and, when getting ready for trips into Lethbridge, they would rent good clothes from a lady who ran a store in the community. Thus, the place became known as Rent 'Em. Wrentham is about 50 km southeast of Lethbridge.

WRITING-ON-STONE PROVINCIAL PARK This park contains Native-carved petroglyphs of men, horses, bows, shields, spears and animals. The name derives from its Cree place name *masinasin*, meaning "rock carvings." For generations, Writing-On-Stone was a place of spiritual importance to the Prairie Natives. The area was designated a provincial park in 1957 and is 43 km east of Milk River.

WYECLIF This hamlet was named after the Wye River Valley in England. Wyeclif is near Edmonton.

Y

YARROW CREEK This creek took its name from the abundance of yarrow weed that grows in the area. Some brew a medicinal tea from this weed. Yarrow Creek is located about 83 km southwest of Lethbridge.

YELLOWHEAD MOUNTAIN (2408 m) This mountain overlooking Yellowhead Pass is located about 33 km west of Jasper. (see Yellowhead Pass)

YELLOWHEAD PASS (1117 m) The Yellowhead Pass, Roche Tête and the BC community of Tête Jaune Cache were named after a person nicknamed *Tête Jaune*, meaning "yellow head." Perhaps this person was blond Iroquois trapper Pierre Hatsinaton. Hatsinaton worked for the Hudson's Bay Company as a guide. Perhaps this person was also known as Pierre Bostonais, another possible namesake for the pass. A third possibility is that the pass was named for François Décoigne, the manager of Jasper House in 1814. (see Robson Pass)

MORE ABOUT YELLOWHEAD PASS… *Yellowhead Pass, 26 km west of Jasper, is the lowest pass through the Canadian Rockies. Travellers approaching the 1133-m pass from the east cross the highest point on the route at Obed, still in the foothills. Sir Sandford Fleming proposed the pass in 1870 as a route through the Rockies for the Canadian Pacific Railway's transcontinental line. Fleming's recommendation was not accepted. Instead the rail line was built through the southern prairies and the higher Kicking Horse Pass (1642 m) and the Rogers Pass (1330 m). Later the "Yellowhead" route was used by the Grand Trunk Pacific Railway and the Canadian Northern Railway. Both of these lines were later taken over by Canadian National Railway. Yellowhead Pass is now also used*

by the inter-provincial Yellowhead Highway. Yellowhead Pass was previously known as Leather Pass, referring to the dressed beaver-skins HBC workers carried over this route. The name of Leather Peak refers to this old name for the pass.

YELLOWSTONE Pop. 97. The origin of the name for this summer village is not known. Yellowstone is located about 63 km west of Edmonton.

YOUNGSTOWN Pop. 239. This village took its name from Joseph V. Young. He owned the land that became the site of this community. Youngstown is about 50 km east-southeast of Hanna.

YOUNGHUSBAND RIDGE This ridge took its name from Lieutenant Colonel Sir Francis Younghusband. He was part of an unsuccessful Mount Everest expedition. The name was put forward in 1927 by A. Ostheimer III, a U.S. alpinist, and officially approved in 1987. Younghusband Ridge is located about 75 km southeast of Jasper.

Y

Z

ZAMA CITY Pop. 217. This hamlet was named after Zama River. The river took its name from Slavey Chief Zama, who travelled the area. Zama City is about 115 km northwest of High Level.

ZIGADENUS LAKE This lake was named for the numerous white camas flowers (of the genus *Zygadenus*) found around its shores. The lake lies 50 km northwest of Banff.

Notes on Sources

Armstrong, G.H. *The Origin and Meaning of Place Names in Canada.* Toronto: MacMillan, 1930.

Atlas of Alberta. Edmonton: Interwest Publications, 1984.

Atlas of Canada. n.p.: Readers' Digest Association (Canada) Limited, 1981.

Canadian Encyclopedia, The. Toronto: McClelland & Stewart, 2000.

City of Edmonton. *Naming Edmonton.* Edmonton: University of Alberta Press, 2004.

Hamilton, William B. *The MacMillan Book of Canadian Place Names.* Toronto: MacMillan of Canada, 1978.

Holmgren, Eric J. and Patricia M. *Over 2000 Place Names of Alberta. Expanded Third Edition.* Saskatoon: Prairie Books, 1976.

Ingles, Ernie B. and N. Merrill Distad. *Peel's Bibliography of the Canadian Prairies to 1953.* Toronto: University of Toronto, 2003.

Karamitsanis et al. *Place Names of Alberta, vols. 1–4.* Calgary: University of Calgary in cooperation with Alberta Community Development and Friends of Geographical Names of Alberta Society, 1991–1996.

Keay, John and Julia Keay. *Collins Encyclopedia of Scotland.* London: HarperCollins, 1994.

MacEwan, Grant. *Fifty Mighty Men.* Saskatoon: Prairie Books, 1975.

MacGregor, James G. *Father Lacombe.* Edmonton: Hurtig, 1975.

Mardon, Ernest G. *Community Names of Alberta.* Lethbridge: University of Lethbridge, 1973.

Rayburn, Alan. *Oxford Dictionary of Canadian Place Names.* Don Mills: Oxford University Press, 1999.

Sanders, Harry M. *The Story Behind Alberta Names. How Cities, Towns, Villages and Hamlets Got Their Names.* Toronto: University of Toronto Press, 1994.

Schäffer, Mary T.S. *A Hunter of Peace: Mary T.S. Schäffer's Old Indian Trails of the Canadian Rockies.* Banff: Whyte Museum of the Canadian Rockies, 1980.

Wouters, Kees and Bob Berube. *Tomorrow It Might Be Gone.* Stony Plain: self-published, 1980.

www.bivouac.com.

www.Spartacus.schoolnet.co.uk.

Fred Katz Studios

Larry Donovan has long been a voice on Alberta's airwaves. From his time with CKUA in the 1980s to his work with CBC Newsworld, he's been telling the important stories for many years. Larry has also contributed to a number of major publications, including the *Financial Times*, the *Financial Times Energy Economist* and the *Globe and Mail*. He also spent time as a broadcaster in England with MonitoRadio in London. He holds a master's degree in environmental management from the University of London. These days, Larry is back in Alberta, and he's returned to his roots with CKUA radio.

Tom Monto is a writer and editor in Edmonton. He moved to the province in his teens, and since then he has been glad to call Alberta home. He's been a journalist, provincial election candidate and amateur scuba diver. Over the last 30 years, Tom has travelled from the southern edges of Alberta to the banks of the Peace River and has visited everywhere from Lloydminster in the east to the

mountains of Jasper in the west. These days, Tom owns Alhambra Books, a rare and second-hand bookstore. He is also a proud dad to his teenage daughter and enjoys working on his hobby farm. Tom has a BA in history and geography from the University of Alberta and has written three books on Alberta history.